Sad, Lonely and A Long Way From Home

A story of marriage and heartbreak

Belinda Conniss

This is my story; of how I came from feeling unloved, to finding romance and a marriage that ended with a battered, broken heart. How I moved from one place to another in search of that kind of love again, which resulted in domestic violence, sexual assault, more heartbreak, and even near death. My story is a roller coaster of highs and lows, but ultimately, it is one of survival.

This is the first book of my life from the age of around 14 to 31, it will continue in a second book, *Secrets and Lies*, from the age of 31 onwards, with a mention throughout both books of my early childhood. As told by me in my own words.

Belinda Conniss

Although this book is based on true events, the names and places have been changed, to protect the identities of some of the people mentioned.

Contents

Introduction 1

1

    Green, Green Grass of Home (1987)...........3

2

    The Hotel....................................12

3

    He Looked at Me with a Warm Smile 22

4

    Kippers for Breakfast....................32

5

    Moving On....................................42

6

    A New Man in My Life..................52

7

    He's Married 57

8

    Lies and Reservations 62

9

    Missing My Daughter 71

10

    Jealously and Suspicion 80

11

A Gun to My Head.........................88

12

The Great Pretender......................95

13

Think Twice.................................105

14

Marriage of Convenience............112

15

Hate in his Eyes...........................121

16

The Journey Back to Scotland 126

17

She's Pregnant 135

18

An Abusive Relationship.............140

19

Back to Wales..............................146

Acknowledgments........................151

Secrets and Lies 153

Introduction

I was born on 11 October 1965 in Govan, Glasgow. My mother was a bus conductress and my dad was unemployed, so times were hard.

We lived in a close, comprising of around eight to ten flats. Obviously, I don't remember much about the flat we lived in except that my cot was in the same room as my parents and the ceiling had a slant.

I was told it was an attic-type dwelling at the top of the tenement. We left there when I was around two-and-a-half-years-old. I have, however, been told stories about Govan and went back there in my mid-40s to see where I came from.

When I was nine-years-old, we moved to a new town that had been developed to house the overspill from Glasgow and Edinburgh. This was our fifth, or maybe sixth, home since I was born, my parents moved around – a lot!

I remember fondly the first day we arrived; it was a brand new home that nobody had lived in before and I was so excited. By this time I have three sisters and a brother so, as you can imagine, in a four bedroom house there was some sharing to do.

I continued to live there until I was 17 when I moved to live with my boyfriend, which was even more exciting, but, looking back, it was an escape from the harsh way that I was brought up.

Being the oldest wasn't always a good thing because I was the one who had to learn fast. I'm not saying it was a terrible childhood, but it sure wasn't great.

I'm not saying that my mother and stepfather didn't love me, but they didn't always show it. If anything, they appeared to resent me, for reasons I found out later on in life.

I believe my childhood and the things that happened to me contributed to why I became a pushover in later years, and was mistreated on several occasions. My early life definitely had a part to play in my future decisions and the things that followed.

1
Green, Green Grass of Home (1987)

My adventures weren't always fun but it was my life and I had to live it. I lived through some hard times and found myself fighting a battle that seemed I was never going to win. I went on a journey to find my true self, and learned that life is what you make it. My struggles took me through the country roads of Wales and back to Scotland twice.

I remember standing in the kitchen listening to Lionel Richie's 'Three times a lady'. How that song would bring back a rush of feelings that were once buried so deep I thought they were gone forever. Now, here I am years' later (playing our song on repeat). This was his song to me, never a fight, nor a frustration. He gave me his everything, his all. He gave me every inch of his heart, until that last year.

He saw me from across the bar as I poured a drink. "I'm going to get that girl," he said, and yes, he did, with those piercing blue eyes and that warm smile that would melt any woman's heart from 100 miles away. In all honesty, I refused him on several occasions, thinking he was like an old song I had heard before. I was just a messed up young girl, and he didn't know what he was letting himself in for.

Then it hit me with full force; I was intrigued by him and it was as if he had put a spell on me. I loved the attention and, if he was really serious, I wanted to see just how long he would wait. He was addictive, as he said the same of me months' later, he made a life full of disappointment so easy to forget. When I was with him I forgot about that bruised young girl I had tried to leave back in Scotland; somehow she didn't exist when he was around. He had this way of erasing every pain and memory.

I remember standing in front of him, our gaze just fixed on each other, the magic could be seen in our eyes; this happiness couldn't be faked, completely enjoying having each other so near. Looking back I still wonder, *was I on the rebound?* And if I was, what did it matter because I fell completely in love with him? He was a charmer and a good one at that, it was years later that I discovered just how good at being charming he really was.

It is with fond memories that I remember all the good times, and yes, we had a few although, sometimes, I found it hard to shake off his uncontrollable temper that surfaced every once in a while. It's funny how you forgive an acid tongue when you're so in love. Who could resist a man with such charm, normally soft spoken words and those blue eyes?

I remember the day I arrived in Wales like it was yesterday. I stepped off the train and walked up the hill to find a taxi. I had had a telephone interview whilst in Scotland for a job in a hotel and got the job that same day. I had been very excited as I packed my case that week and sold all my personal possessions to pay for my ticket; with butterflies in my tummy like a child who had just seen Father Christmas. There were no taxis to be found when I reached the top of the hill so, suitcase in hand, I started to walk to the nearest village.

A small, beautiful village awaited my arrival and I will never forget how stunning it was. The weather was lovely that day, the sun beamed in my face and there was only a hint of a breeze. I walked along the endless path which, looking back, reminded me of *The Green Mile*, a movie I watched years later, with green as far as the eye could see and beautiful flower beds dotted here and there. As I crossed the road I could see a pub, I walked over and in I went, full of nerves. I walked over to the bar and I could feel everyone in the entire pub's eyes upon me. *Oh dear*, I thought, *how quiet it became when I walked in.* It was a couple of months later that I came to understand why this happens. When you walk into a shop or a pub and people immediately put up their defences, it is because to them you are an outsider and it's a case of, "Who is this? Why is she here? What does she want?" *Strange people*, I thought as I asked the bar lady where I could get a taxi to take me to the Silver Fox Hotel?

"Ah," she said, "you can call one from here. Are you a newcomer?"

"Yes, I have travelled down from Scotland."

"Let me pour some drinks, then I will drive you." *Oh okay*, I thought, *friendly lady*.

We got into the car and set off; it was a couple of miles drive so I was very pleased of the lift. As we drove there the song that was playing on the radio was Tom Jones 'Green, Green Grass of Home'. I liked Tom Jones and sang along in my head. The woman started to chat, asking me what had brought me to Wales. I'm not the sort of person to tell people about my personal life so I just said I fancied a change.

"Well," she said, "there's no better place to do that than Wales, you'll like it here."

As the car pulled into the car park I sat there in awe. I could not believe the stunning views and I thought to myself, *this may be just what I need, I think I'm going to like it here.* The hotel was beautiful, a proper old country hotel in the middle of the hills. Who would have thought that there was a stunning village and just a short drive away there was all this beautiful scenery?

As I opened the door and walked in I was taken aback by the sheer beauty of the interior of the hotel and by the warmth and quietness. I rang the bell on the counter and a lady came through a door just behind the reception.

"Hi," she said, "do you have a reservation?"

"No," I replied, "I'm looking for Alison, my name is Belinda and I spoke to her on the telephone from Scotland."

"Oh," she said, "hi, Belinda, I'm Alison and I am very pleased to meet you! It's nice to put a face to the voice. You must be very tired after such a long journey."

"Yes, I am." I had been travelling for around five hours by now and I was a little tired, cold and stiff because I had been sitting for so long.

"Well," Alison continued, "I have your room ready so I will take you up. Then you can unpack and have a couple of hours rest. We have evening meals between 5 and 8.00 p.m. and after you've eaten I will show you around." Gosh, was I pleased that everything was ready for me; I couldn't wait to have a nap.

I woke up around six o'clock feeling quite peckish and, after having a shower and getting dressed, I went down for some food. As I got closer to the kitchen my stomach began to rumble as the aroma from the kitchen was something else. *Mmmm,* I thought, *it smells good.* As I entered the kitchen there were a couple of girls rushing around, another at the sink and the chef was by the cooker.

"Hi, you must be Belinda? Come in and have a seat, we have a choice of trout with mushrooms, venison pie or steak Diane?"

I opted for the trout. It was lovely, I hadn't tried trout before but I enjoyed every bit. Alison arrived a little later, once everything had calmed down, and introduced me to everyone. "Belinda, this is our chef, Antonio. He's the best chef around and we wouldn't know what to do without him." Antonio was around five feet seven, with dark hair and a medium build and spoke with a French accent. He seemed pleasant enough. "By the sink we have Claire," Now, I thought, *isn't she small...* She was around four feet nine, perhaps slightly taller, an English girl with short hair. "And this is Elaine, our longest serving staff member and very good at her job."

"Pleased to meet you," I said. Elaine was a very tall girl, olive skinned with long jet black hair, and a medium build. It's funny because I have always believed that you should never judge a person until you know them and yet, here I was making my own snap assessment of the people I was being introduced to.

I can usually tell within the first five minutes of speaking to someone if I'm going to like them but, in saying that, I have often taken a dislike to someone only to end up their best friend once I get to know them.

Alison gave me a tour of the hotel and explained what my duties would be. "We have a rota here, Belinda, and most of the time you will be paired up with one of the other girls, unless we are short staffed. You will start at 6.00 a.m., preparing breakfasts in the kitchen and our guests come down between seven and nine. The tables are always set the night before, after all the guests have had their evening meal."

"Cool," I said.

"You can have breakfast after all the washing up is done, unless you are in early enough to have it before you start. You, and whoever you are paired with, will have twelve rooms to clean. That will take you up lunchtime, around one thirty/two o'clock, and you can then have a one hour break. After lunch, you may be required to help out in the bar and then it is back in the kitchen by 5:00 p.m. for the evening meals, after which you can have yours.

"When you finish at 8:00 p.m., I would like you to work in the bar with Elaine. Last orders are at 11:00 p.m. but sometimes we have a lock-in, in which case we will try to get you finished as early as possible as you will be up early in the morning. Lock-ins usually happen on two or three nights and they finish around 3:00 a.m. If you are in the bar until that time, you will start at ten the next morning."

Wow, I thought, just listening to all that makes me feel exhausted and I haven't even started my first shift yet.

"You will work a six day week with one day off. Look at the rota to see what day you have been allocated. If, for any reason, you need another day off, or if you have an appointment, you can see if one of the girls can swap with you unless you know the week before and I can fit that in for you. Some of the girls, like yourself, come from another part of the country and would like to go home from time to time and that can be arranged quickly if it's an emergency, otherwise you will need to save your holidays; your entitlement is one and a half days for every full month worked. Your board and food is taken care of but you will pay for your uniform. You remember what you're monthly salary is?"

"Yes, I do thanks," I replied.

"Okay, any questions just fire away? Oh, and if you work overtime it goes into the book and we pay you in your next month's salary are you okay with that?"

I nodded. Yes, Alison, that's great thanks.

Well, Belinda you have had a long day travelling and we would like you to settle in over the next couple of days. Your first full shift will begin Monday, so tomorrow you can pair up with Claire. Just familiarise yourself with what she is doing and maybe lend a hand, so you can get the hang of things. You will be paid for tomorrow even though you're just doing a couple of hours. Claire will also show you around the village on Sunday as that's her day off. I have you down for a day off on Wednesday which is the same day as Elaine so, she can take you down to register with the doctor's and dentist's surgeries and anything else you would like to do.

"My shift is over for the night, so if I don't see you tomorrow I will see you six o'clock on Monday, good-night." Wow, there was no messing around as far as Alison was concerned, she was straight to the point then out the door!

2
The Hotel

Gosh! I slept like a log last night, I thought, as I awoke to the sound of the birds and the sun glaring through the window of my room. I woke up at six thirty which was lovely because it meant I had most of the day to myself, except for the couple of hours I would work with Claire getting used to my duties.

I had a very good feeling about my future in Wales, a new challenge lay ahead and it was time to start over. Nobody knew me and I could just be myself. I got into the shower, which was so refreshing at that time in the morning, got dressed and had a cup of tea and a biscuit to keep me going until I went downstairs.

It was such a pleasure to sit back, enjoy my breakfast and observe everything that was going on around me. At the same time, I chatted with Antonio about the hotel and the staff.

Claire rushed back and forth with guests' breakfasts. "Belinda," she said, after your breakfast feel free to walk around the grounds of the hotel, it's such a warm day. We won't be able to start the rooms until ten anyway and it will save you sitting around waiting for me."

"Oh, okay," I said, "it looks lovely outside, thanks."

Walking around the grounds of the hotel was so beautiful, with the sun shining and that warm glow in my face with only a hint of a breeze, just as it had been when I arrived the day before. The scenery was magical and the hotel was surrounded by hills and the most spectacular views. It's funny, though, because we have all this in Scotland yet I didn't seem to appreciate it when I was there, which is something I came to regret later. I could hear voices which got louder, as I approached the pond situated at the bottom of the huge garden, and when I say huge, I mean huge. I had never before seen a garden that big.

"What the hell do you mean, you didn't know, how stupid are you? I told you I didn't know the woman, so go f**k yourself."

Oh my God, what on earth is going on? I thought, as I heard all of this shouting. I tried to keep from being spotted because I wasn't sure what was coming next. Then I heard something smash and, as I looked over the hedge, I could see a man and a woman hurling abuse at one another. The shouting got worse and then the woman threw, what looked like, a glass across the garden. Smash! At that point I felt it best to hurry back to the kitchen.

"Antonio," I said breathlessly. "I'm afraid you have a couple of guests shouting and smashing things in the garden." Antonio started to laugh, so much so he was holding his sides.

"Oh, Belinda, my dear girl, I'm afraid you will have to get used to that!"

"What do you mean?" I replied. "Does this happen often?" His laugh got louder and by this time he was almost on his knees.

I looked on, puzzled, but at the same time with a smirk because Antonio had laughed so hard.

"That is Penny and Paulo."

"Who are Penny and Paulo?" I asked.

Antonio looked at me and said through his laughter, "Penny is the owner of the hotel and Paulo is her husband."

"What? You mean they behave like this when running a business? Do they do this in front of the guests?" I said in astonishment.

Antonio still laughing, replied, "Belinda that is mild compared to their behaviour at other times. You'll see soon enough."

And that I did! I'm talking scary stuff. I remember another time their argument involved a gun which frightened me because I actually thought someone was going to be killed. Antonio poured me a cup of tea. I think he felt sorry for me because I had only just arrived and all hell had broken loose. He must have wondered if I was thinking *what have I let myself in for?* I wasn't thinking that at all but I did think it strange that the owner of the hotel would fight like that right under the windows of the guests' rooms. It was an odd situation. *Oh well,* I thought, *let's see what the rest of the day brings.*

Claire called me from the other end of the kitchen, "Belinda, I'm just going to grab a bite to eat then we can go upstairs to make a start on the rooms."

"No problem," I said, "I'll go have a look around the front of the hotel and come back to meet you."

There were fourteen rooms in the hotel but only twelve had to be cleaned. There was no number thirteen? I asked Claire why this was and she explained that hotels don't have a room 13 because it's an unlucky number. Well, I didn't know that before. Claire told me that we also didn't clean room 1 as that was the room that Paulo slept in.

"Paulo's room? Why on earth would he not be in the apartment downstairs with his wife?" I enquired.

"Well, it's a long story but to cut it short they don't get on. Penny wants a divorce and Paulo won't do it, so he has been banished to room 1 so that he is out of her way." *Well,* I thought, *this just gets better and better.*

Claire explained that room 14 only was only cleaned every couple of weeks because it was haunted and none of the girls liked to clean it as they said they heard things in there.

"I don't mind doing it…as long as someone is with me," Claire added, "because I think there is definitely something strange in there." *Oh no, please don't tell me anymore,* I thought, *I don't know if I can handle that.* I'm not a fan of ghost stories.

Claire filled me in on the Penny and Paulo story, as I didn't want to put my foot in it with either of them about who I reported to.

"You answer to Alison, she is the manager and deals with all the shifts, the rota, hours and wages. She also oversees the workload and that it's done to satisfaction," said Claire. "Penny is the owner and she just likes to plod along and not be disturbed. She comes and goes, but Alison does report to her on a daily basis to let her know everything is running smoothly. You may even find that Penny will chat a little if you are in the same room as her. As for Paulo, I would watch with him, he is a bit of a ladies man and may hover around you. Any bother from him though, or if he makes you feel uncomfortable, make sure you report it to Alison otherwise he may get you sacked."

Claire went on to explain that there was a girl who worked there and Paulo was having a thing with her as he did with a few of the girls. The girl just went along with it to keep him sweet because he was the owner's husband, but she soon regretted it because Alison found out and had it out with Paulo. He denied everything and said that the girl had kept pestering him and wouldn't take no for an answer, so Alison had fired her.

"So make sure you try and keep any conversation with him to a minimum," said Claire, "I would also make sure that you double lock your room at night. He may try to come up and annoy you and, if he doesn't get an answer, he may even have the pass key with him and try to come into your room."

"Oh my God, your serious?" I said, disheartened, "I'm beginning to wonder if I should have taken this job."

"Don't feel too bad, you'll be fine, and if you're worried or scared if anything does happen just go straight to Alison, because then if he tries to make out you done something wrong at least you will already have been to her first."

"Thanks for the advice Claire," I said, "I will make sure he doesn't get within a foot of me."

No sooner than Claire and I had had our chat, along came Paulo to meet the new girl.

"Well, well," he said, "and what have we here?" As soon as I heard him speak I thought *Uh! French...* "Well, Claire, are you going to introduce me to our new recruit?"

"Paulo, this is Belinda. She is from Scotland and I'm showing her the ropes before she starts on Monday."

"Well, hello, Belinda, I hope you will like it here. So, you're from Scotland, a place I have never been. They say it is beautiful and by the look of you they have all the pretty ladies too." *Yuk*, I thought, *what a disgusting man.*

"Yes, it is very beautiful, but then so is Wales, and I'm sure the ladies are as pretty here as they are in Scotland."

"Oh, I don't know about that," said Paulo. "I have seen some very ugly ladies in my time." *Oh my God*, I thought to myself, *this man is so rude, no wonder his wife don't want him to stay in the same apartment as her.*

"I will be in the bar tonight at 6:00p.m., come, please, I will buy you a drink to welcome you, Belinda."

"Maybe," I said, "if I'm not too busy." *Anything to get rid of him,* I thought.

Claire said that I didn't have to go if you didn't want to but that she would be finishing at six because she had worked two late nights, and could meet me in the bar.

"Have one drink from him," she said, "then you and I will go to the Hole in the Wall."

"What's that?" I asked.

"It's a little bed and breakfast-cum-pub only five minutes' walk from here," said Claire. "You'll like it; the people are friendly and I will introduce you to Jeff and Dave, a couple of my friends. They sing there on Friday and Saturday nights and they are good."

"Sounds like a plan," I agreed. "Yes, let's do that."

We had cleaned a couple of rooms when Claire said, "Okay, Belinda, give me a hand with room 14, then you shoot off for a couple of hours rest before you get ready to meet me tonight."

Room 14 was as eerie as Claire had described it. I don't know if this was because I expected to hear or see something, or if it was actually haunted. Still, I didn't like the feel of the room and it was so cold in there. I asked Claire why people thought the room was haunted.

"Well, I'm not sure how true the story is because it was before I came to work here but they say someone died in there."

"Oh dear," I replied. "Maybe it's just the thought that someone died that makes it seem so eerie when people talk about it."

"I don't know," Claire said, "but I sure as hell ain't staying long enough to find out. I just come in quick, hoover and dust and that's it because nobody actually stays in the room now.

When I dust, I leave the hoover running so that's all I can hear to be on the safe side." I laughed when she said that and, at the same time, I thought, *well, that's exactly what I shall do when I have to clean it.*

Back in my room I decided what I was going to wear that night. I'm quite vain. I'm not an oil painting but I'm sure not ugly either and I have legs women would die for, so I always like to look my best. I was actually looking forward to a night out, mainly because I was going to see a little more of the village.

I made a couple of phone calls back home just to let everyone know I was okay and everything was looking good. There was one person I was itching to call but knew if I did it would cause problems so I had to leave it for now.

I chose a lovely black pencil skirt and a white cotton blouse with my court shoes. I loved to wear pencil skirts because it showed off my figure…Yep! I had an amazing figure considering I had given birth to my first child, a daughter, four and a half years earlier.

I know you must be wondering, 'A daughter? Four and a half years ago? So where is she now?' Well, that will all come to light soon enough.

Looking at myself in the mirror, blusher brush in hand, I felt a sense of happiness that I hadn't felt in a long time, but still the ache in my heart wouldn't shift. It was always there, no matter how good I felt. It remained sizzling away in the background, waiting to resurface when my guard was down.

3
He Looked at Me with a Warm Smile

There was a knock on my room door! *Oh no* I thought, *please God don't let it be Paulo.*

"Belinda… are you ready?" It was Claire. I looked at my watch; it was six thirty. Oh no, I had been so busy thinking about my daughter, I forgot all about the time.

"Yes, hold on. I will open the door."

"What have you been doing? Your half an hour late?"

"Oh, I'm sorry, Claire, I dozed off. I didn't realise I had slept so long."

"Well, never mind, I will wait for you. You'll only be another few minutes, yes?"

"Yep, I'll be ready in a flash." There was no way I could tell her what had really happened, I wanted to avoid any questions about my daughter. In fact, I didn't want anyone to know about her, well not yet anyway.

There was a lovely atmosphere in the bar, and a warm welcoming feeling which I was glad of as there was a cold chill in the air outside as the evening drew in. There was a wonderful coal fire burning which was so cosy I could have sat there all night. What with the heat from the fire and a couple of glasses of cherry brandy I had a warm glow. Paulo was there when we arrived with that kind of 'dirty old man' look on his face.

I said to Claire, "This man disgusts me and I don't like French men, they are vile."

Claire laughed, "Don't be put you off because of one man, Belinda, they're not all like that." "Oh yes, they are, Claire, trust me." I was going by what I had seen on the television and from what I had heard other people say. I know that's probably naive but when I get an idea into my head I'm not usually far wrong.

The door of the bar opened and in walked four strapping lads, but there was one who caught my eye. He was tall and tanned, of medium build with dark hair and shiny eyes. They all looked across at the table at me, Claire and Paulo were sitting at. The one who I had noticed, gave me such a handsome smile showing off his white teeth, I smiled back then looked away as I could feel my face going red.

"Oh La, said Claire, It looks like you have got the attention of Barry.

"Yes, so who's Barry, then?"

"The one with the tanned skin who just smiled at you."

"Gosh, Claire," I laughed, "you don't miss a trick do you?"

"Nope," she replied.

"Well, I was just being polite, although I have to say he is rather dishy."

Claire laughed, "Belinda, many a girl has caught the eye of Barry and many have wanted to be his girlfriend but it's never happened."

"Why," I asked, "is he gay?" At that, Claire let out such a loud laugh that the whole pub turned around and wondered what was going on.

"No," she said, "he's not gay, he is just choosy about who he dates. I have seen him with a couple of stunners in my time but none that have lasted very long. I'm afraid it takes a special kind of gal to keep Barry from straying."

"Ah, so he's one of those ladies' men, oh well, I know not to go there then, 'cause I too, am choosy about who gets to date me and it's no ladies' man, or ugly man, that's for sure," I said, making sure that Paulo heard every word in the hope that he would't even try.

"Well, let's get going. I have a couple of friends for you to meet and they have our drinks waiting for us," said Claire.

"Where are you two going then?" asked Paulo?

"We are off to the Hole in the Wall," said Claire.

"Oh, I come with you then, and I look after you for the evening."

Claire thanked him but said that we were meeting friends and that we would be fine. I could see he was not amused and, although I didn't want him there either, I did feel a little sorry for him. But then, that's me; I feel sorry for everyone and try not to upset the apple cart. As we made our way to the door I could see Barry's eyes staring right through me, with a smile on his face. I kindly smiled back and we left.

It was a beautiful evening but a little nippy, as we walked along a peaceful and quiet country road, with hills on one side. We passed a farm with derelict buildings on the other.

"Claire," I said, "why has that building been left like that?"

This is Tom the farmers building. It's sad when they leave them to rot but it costs too much to repair.

"Gosh, I would buy that and have it done up. It would make a beautiful cottage."

"Yes, it would, and you know Tom has been made offers many times by potential buyers but he always says no. He would rather hold on to it than sell it, even though it's getting ruined."

"That's a shame," I said.

"You'll meet Tom on Monday morning, he comes in for Antonio to cook him breakfast and in return he takes away all the food scraps for his pigs."

"I'll look forward to that."

"Maybe not, he stinks," laughed Claire. I almost choked when she said that and asked why she would say that about him.

"Because he is a farmer and all farmers stink, you'll see when he comes," she replied.

I had never met a farmer before because I came from a town, and was born in a city, so it was a new thing to me and I enjoyed the stories I had been told over the years about farmers and their way of life. I asked Claire about Antonio as he had been very quiet when I met him but seemed pleasant enough when I spoke to him.

"Antonio is French," Claire said, "and a wonderful chef, and for as long as he has been here I have never seen him with a woman. Elaine says he is gay but we will never know because he doesn't discuss his private life." *Well, I thought, I can identify with because neither do I.*

"Here we are then," said Claire, "this is the Hole in the Wall." *Thank goodness,* I thought. I was out of breath from walking up the hill and also quite cold.

As soon as we opened the door I could feel the heat from the coal fire which made me smile. *Great,* I thought, *another blazing fire.* As we walked towards the table I could hear whispers from the locals. I didn't need the brain of Einstein to figure out what they were saying.

Claire introduced me to her friends. "Jeff, Dave, this is Belinda. She is from Scotland and has come to work at The Silver Fox." They both stood up and shook my hand.

"Pleased to meet you, Belinda, here is your cherry brandy."

"Oh, thank you, but how did you know that's what I drink?"

"Claire called us earlier to tell us to have the drinks ready, she's a bossy little thing." We all laughed and sat down. We chatted for what seemed like hours. Jeff and Dave were a couple of musicians who played in various bars on different evenings of the week. They played at The Silver Fox on Fridays and Saturdays and sometimes one night during the week, although they hadn't that weekend as they had just come back from holiday

I discovered, as the night went on, that Claire had feelings for Jeff and hoped that one day he and she would date each other. Sadly, it was plain to see he didn't feel the same way. Claire appeared not to have noticed, or perhaps she did and simply wished that he would like her.

Jeff and Dave were both from London. We talked a lot about Scotland as they had never been there, so I was questioned most of the night about different places and events, including Edinburgh Castle and the Military Tattoo.

"Tell us about the Castle, Belinda, and the Tattoo," they said. Well what could I say?

"The castle? Mmmm, well when you have seen one, you have seen them all. As far as I know the castle sits on top of a volcano! And the Tattoo, well I have never been but it's just a load of men in skirts who play the drums and the bagpipes." The truth of the matter was that I didn't really know because I have little memory of when I was last at the castle and I have never been to the Tattoo as it's not something that interests me.

"Wow," said Jeff, "you're a true Scot and yet you know little of your heritage."

That was very true, I thought to myself, but then history was never my strong point and I hated the bagpipes. Or at least I did until that moment when I realised there was such a lot I had missed out on back home. It was at that moment I promised myself I would learn more about where I came from.

"What an interesting night," I said to Claire later, "thanks for taking me along, and what lovely lads Jeff and Dave are."

"Well, you wait until next weekend and you hear them singing, they are really good."

"I'm looking forward to it," I replied. "Gosh, its cold now what time is it?"

"Eleven thirty! Still time for a last drink in The Silver Fox before we head to bed I reckon?" I quickly agreed. I needed to warm up by that coal fire before I went to my room.

As we entered everyone looked round and I mean, everyone! The bar was full with hardly any room to move. As we went closer to the fire, I felt someone brush past me and then apologise. As I looked round to say that's okay, I felt my face go red, it was Barry. He looked at me with a warm smile and asked, "Did you have a good night, Belinda?"

"How do you know my name?" I said.

"Ah well, us locals make it our business to know who is coming and going, and with a little luck you won't be going." I blushed when he said that and didn't know what to reply. "Belinda," Claire shouted, "what do you want to drink?"

"I'll get that," said Barry.

"Gosh, I'm popular tonight," I said with a smile, "I could get used to this."

"Belinda, you have got the prettiest smile and, I hope you don't mind me saying, you have the most beautiful eyes." I wasn't surprised that he commented on my eyes as they seem to be my best feature. Lots of people, including women, have noticed them over the years. I have to admit though, they are pretty; sky blue, and can be quite piercing in the right light.

It became quite evident by his body language that Barry liked me, and he was a looker I'll say that. He had just come back from an overseas holiday, hence the olive skin. He did look rather dashing and had such a lovely smile too.

I was becoming quite tired. I had been up since six thirty, then helped Claire for a few hours before sitting and drinking for most of the night and, with little to eat, so I wasn't doing myself any favours.

"I think I will go up to bed now, Claire," I said sleepily. "I'm struggling to keep my eyes open and tomorrow Elaine is taking me into the village."

"It's called Bryn Deri, Belinda. You will like it there."

"Good, I'm looking forward to it. Well I'm off, I will catch up with you later and thanks again for tonight." I turned to Barry, "Thank you for the drink, it was lovely to meet you."

"Oh you're welcome, Belinda. I'm looking forward to doing it again. I'm glad you enjoyed yourself."

As I got up to leave, Barry came over to me whispered, "Belinda, maybe some time when you're not too busy I can take you out and show you around."

"Yes, maybe, I'm not sure when my day off is but I'm sure I will see you in here anyway."

Sounds good, well, I will see you soon. 'Goodnight Barry'

"Sleep tight beautiful."

A part of me felt warm and loved for being the focus of attention, but another part of me was still mending a broken heart, so I didn't want to start dating anyone, certainly not yet.

I was glad that I was heading up to bed.

"Belinda," Claire shouted after me as I was walking up the stairs.

"What's wrong?"

She came closer and whispered, "Remember what I said about double locking your room door, Paulo is still in the bar he may try to come up."

Oh, no way, that's all I need, I thought.

"Yep, I will, Claire, thank you," I said, And goodnight.

4
Kippers for Breakfast

I couldn't believe the weekend went by so quickly, but then you know what they say, 'time flies when you're having fun'. I had a lovely day with Elaine who showed me the places of interest and those that might be useful or I might like, although I couldn't help feeling that she felt it a burden to have to show me around. It was just the way she spoke and the things she talked about. She told me to watch out for Claire, as she was two faced. Well, I had found her to be a very pleasant girl who was bags of fun and full of laughter. I personally think that Elaine may have been a little jealous of Claire because she was small and petite and everyone loved her. However, I made the best of the day, and enjoyed another evening drinking in the bar.

I was in the shower at ten past five in the morning and must admit, I had a wonderful sleep, probably because of the alcohol I drank the night before. After my cup of tea and biscuit I headed down to the kitchen. I had to wear black and white until my uniform arrived, so I kept a spare skirt and blouse for the job.

"Well," said Antonio, "don't you look very smart this morning up, with the birds and ready to go."

"That's Me Antonio, the early bird catches the worm." He laughed and said he liked that.

I started taking breakfast plates through to the dining room to the guests and couldn't help but notice most were American and Canadian, and what an unusual breakfast they had; some had kippers and iced tea, others had pancakes with syrup and some had both. Oh dear, I loved kippers but not for breakfast and the smell was so strong. The amount of times I served kippers over time has put me off them for life; now I can't even bear to smell them let alone eat them.

They seemed nice people though; very chatty and left very good tips which we would leave in a jar until the end of the week and share between us all.

After breakfast was finished I had time for my mine which was poached eggs on toast, and a lovely cup of tea. It went down a treat and I thanked Antonio very much. I could hear someone shouting and as the sound got closer, I thought it must be Penny and Paulo at it again, but no, it was Tom the farmer, the one Claire had told me about.

Antonio had already cooked Tom's breakfast and asked me to serve it to him. Well, the smell when I got closer made me hold my breath. I knew then what Claire was talking about. I have to say though, he was a lovely man, very talkative and lively. We became good friends actually.

He said to me, "Belinda, I have a friend who lives in Pinewood." (A village in the opposite direction to where I had been the day before.) "His name is Monty and he is from your neck of the woods. You look out for him when you go to Pinewood and be sure to introduce yourself, as you come from the same place."

"I sure will, thanks, Tom. It's my day off on Wednesday," I said. "I will see if I can get there." "Make sure you tell him Tom sent you," he replied.

Sure enough, Monty was a lovely man; a typical Glaswegian and there was no messing when he was around, I reckon there was quite a few who wouldn't want to upset him. We were friends for five years before sadly, he passed away. I always remember him having a lump on his neck and when I got to know him better I told him he should go see the doctor as it was growing. He just used to laugh and say it was his extra brain. Turned out it was cancer. I was quite upset when he died because we became quite close and he did indeed look after me. If anyone as much as looked at me the wrong way he was on it.

Pinewood was a nice little village and I made some lovely friends there too, I played pool in a little pub called The Oak. Jeff and Dave sang there and Claire was right, they sure did know how to sing. I loved their songs, and when we had the lock-ins at The Silver Fox we would all sit round singing along to the music. 'American Pie' was one of my favourites and they used to sing a lot of Irish songs as well like 'Wild Rover', another favourite, which I enjoyed probably because I have Irish blood.

One night on my evening off, I decided to stay at The Silver Fox rather than go to Pinewood and have a few drinks. Claire and I would sing along to the songs and have a rare old time. We got a lot of attention and I enjoyed every bit of it. Barry came in that night and asked me if he could take me out for a drink to a place called Ebbw Vale.

"Yes, that sounds good."

"I'm off on Friday, if you fancy it then?"

"That will be fine because I'm not working on Saturday."

"I'll pick you up about seven o'clock, that will give me time to get in from work and get ready."

"That's great," I said, "I will meet you in here."

"I hope I may bump into you before then as well," said Barry.

I didn't think it would be a problem to go out for a drink, after all I was a newcomer getting to know the people and the places. I would make it clear to Barry that I wasn't looking to date anyone, assuming that's what he had in mind.

I lay in bed that night unable to sleep for a while, running through my head all I had done in that first couple of weeks in Wales and how nice the Welsh people were. (Although I did also think that I should give up drinking, but when I did drink it made me forget the pain of what I had left behind. Many months later, I realised that when I was sober the pain was still there and I was still very much a broken girl!)

I thought I heard a noise outside the room. I lay there listening and yes, again, I heard a light tap. It was a knock on my room door. *Oh no*, I thought, *please God don't let that be Paulo!* There was one more knock and then nothing. *Thank heavens for that* I thought, *he has gone away* but no sooner had I said that than I heard a key in the door. By this time my heart was pounding. I was sure that I had double locked it. *Please God, I'm too afraid to get up, please let that double lock be on.*

A few minutes went by; nothing! He must have got the message and left. Not long after, the phone in my room started ringing.

I picked it up and said quietly, "Hello…"

"Hello, Belinda," said the voice, "why I come to your room to see you are okay and you do not open the door?"

Oh my God…It was Paulo! I couldn't believe he would go so far as to call my room in the middle of the bloody night.

"Paulo, is that you?" I asked, pretending to have just woke up.

"Yes, Belinda, please I come to see that everything is well for you, yes?"

"Everything is fine, thank you, Paulo, but I was asleep. I have to get up early in the morning. I can't let you come to my room. I will see you tomorrow."

Before he could answer, I hung up the phone. I was raging, what a bloody cheek! Who the hell did he think he was? I must have nodded off soon after because that was the last thing I remember.

I had been working and living in The Silver Fox now for a few months and everyday seemed like the same old boring routine, although I was happy in my job in that I got to make some wonderful friends and have lots of fun. By now Paulo had got the hint and given up on me but not before we had had a few words one morning in the bar when we were alone. "Belinda," he said, "why when I want to speak to you, I find it hard to do so and why, when I come to your room, you do not let me in. Are you afraid of me?"

"No, Paulo," I said, "I'm not afraid of you but I do wonder why you want to come to my room?" I knew exactly what he wanted, but I pretended that I was a little dumb.

"I like you, Belinda, I think you must know that, you are a very beautiful lady and I want us to be friends."

"Paulo, I don't know about where you come from, but where I am from friends do not come to each other's rooms in the middle of the night, why do you do that? If I were Penny I would not be happy with my husband going to young ladies rooms at night."

"I am sorry, Belinda, I just want to talk. Penny and I do not live together, so why would that bother you?"

"Oh, Paulo, you just don't get it, do you? Please don't come to my room at night anymore. I will be your friend but at work only, not outside of work."

I found out later that Paulo and Elaine had been having an affair for quite some time and that disgusted me. It wasn't Claire I had to watch out for, it was Elaine and she was trouble with a capital 'T'.

Alison came into the kitchen one morning and said to me, "Okay, Belinda, you've been living in the hotel for a few months now and we have a room ready for you at the bedsit, only trouble is you will have to share with Jane." Jane was the girl who took the guests on tours but she had found another job and was working her notice.

"Great," I said, When can I move in?"

"Jane goes home at the end of the month so you can either move in and share for now or wait until the end of the month."

"I will move in right away," I replied, "if that's okay with you." I had a good motive; I wanted out of that hotel room away from Paulo as quickly as possible.

"Yep, no problem, I will ask her to make room for you and you can move in tomorrow as it's your day off."

Barry was in the bar that night and asked if I needed help to shift my things, I didn't have a lot to move, but I said yes anyway. He was a nice lad, Barry, and by now we had spent quite a lot of time together, and had a few nights. I did like him, he was so handsome and yes, we had shared a few kisses.

We moved my stuff in the next morning and Barry helped me to get everything settled.

"Well," he said, "this is nice, and you will have a little more freedom to do what you want to do now."

"I will," I replied, "and come the end of the month the room will be mine as Jane is moving out."

Jane was a weird girl she was having an affair with a local man who was already married and had a child. He was also a friend of Paulo and there were another couple of men they were friendly with. The four together were a lethal combination. They all had children and they all thought they were God's gift. They liked to put it about and, although they were all married, it didn't seem to bother them that they were sleeping around. I didn't much care for any of them.

I didn't much care for Jane either because I didn't like the fact that she was dating a married man, but we had to share a room and get on with it. I think she was annoyed as well, because whenever her man came she had to go out or hope that I was going out so they could be alone. Not me, though, as much as I hated it, I stayed put. Maybe if her man had been single, I might have given her the space she needed.

Not long after I moved into the bedsit, I took ill. Jane had gone to stay in the other room as Claire had gone home for the weekend. I awoke in the middle of the night unable to breathe. I had my left arm against my left ribcage and was struggling for breath, it seemed as though I was like that for hours because I couldn't shout for help. It was four thirty in the morning when Jane came into the room for her clothes for work that day. She switched on the light and found me there in that state.

"Oh, my God, what's wrong with you? Belinda, tell me what's up?" I couldn't speak, couldn't even move, so she ran out of the room. Minutes later, I could hear someone running up the stairs. It was Paulo and Jane, they burst into the room and Paulo took one look at me and told Jane to call the doctor. By the time the doctor got there my breathing was getting worse. He gave me an injection then called the hospital.

He told me, "Belinda, you will have to go into hospital." After examining me, he said I had pleurisy. My breathing started to calm down as a result of whatever he injected me with. I told him that I wasn't going into hospital and that I would be fine.

"I can't make you go," he said, "but you will need someone get this prescription for you. And this condition means that you won't be able to work for the next seven to ten days."

5
Moving On

I woke up a couple of mornings later to the sun shining and I did feel better, so I decided to go and sit outside in the garden to read my book. There I was sitting in the sun, on a lovely warm day, and enjoying the relaxation. What I didn't realise was that I was getting worse and the next morning I woke to the pain all over again, only this time I thought I was dying.

Jane ran to tell Paulo and they called an ambulance. Jane said later that I was going grey and they knew I needed help badly. I ended up in hospital for a week with tubes and drips attached to me all over the place.

The nurse sat beside me and explained that I had pleurisy and pneumonia and I was very lucky they found me when they did or I might not be here today. I guess I had a lot to thank Jane for, but unfortunately she had moved back home by the time I was out of hospital. It turned out that she had fallen pregnant by that married man and he wanted nothing more to do with her.

Things had started to get a little heavy with Barry by now, and he said he wanted us to be a proper couple because he felt every time we kissed he was falling for me more and more. It made me sad that I had to tell him it wasn't going to happen, although I wasn't that blunt. I let him down gently and told him I wanted to remain friends. I still felt sad because I did really like him but I wasn't ready for a long-term relationship, at least not until I had dealt with the situation I left back in Scotland. He was a little upset but did get over it and we have been friends ever since. In fact I was at his wedding years later. I also became good friends with his wife.

A few months later, Claire and I went to the Hole in the Wall for a drink because Jeff and Dave were playing, and what a great night it was. I was rather tipsy and feeling quite jolly, hence why I said yes to Jeff when he asked me out. Now, Jeff I would never have taken as being my type so, to this day, I still don't understand why I said yes. He was about five feet nine with shoulder length black curly hair. I can't imagine what I was thinking back then!

However, we did have a couple of lovely nights out but after that I had to tell him that I wasn't really looking for a relationship. We did remain friends, though. Well, up until he had a gun shoved in his face and was told to move back to where he came from, but more of that later!

I decided it was time for a change and so I started looking for another job. I felt Alison was starting to rely on me for duties other than the ones I had already and it just didn't suit me to have her put my name down for every job in the hotel. The trouble with me, is I'm a grafter. I will work my socks off and will do for others all too easily, but that soon showed me that people will use me if they can get away with it. I ended up working more than my fair share of hours. With little sleep, the body can only take so much before it tells you to slow down or stop.

I became friendly with Alexandra, the girl who worked at the vets in Bryn Deri; she was a nice girl but could be a little eccentric. I told her I was looking for another job and a place to stay. "Well, Belinda," she said. "It just so happens that I have a spare room and I could do with a little extra money!" *Wow, how lucky I am?* I thought I asked when I could move in.

"As soon as you like," she said. "You can start paying me when you find another job, there's no rush."

I arranged to move in the following week. I took Alison to the side and told her I was working my notice.

"What," she said, surprised. "Why? I thought you were happy here."

"I am, Alison, and I can't thank you enough for your generosity. I have loved working here and made so many lovely friends but I feel I need a change. I work so many hours and I'm tired. I need a less stressful job." Alison said that she would look at the rota and try to change things, as they were short staffed since Jane left. By then, Claire had left also because her mother was poorly she decided to move back home.

"I'm sorry, Alison," I said, "but it will be some time before you get new staff I feel I need to go now. I plan to leave at the end of the month. I'll write my notice and give it to you in the morning."

"If you're sure," she replied, "but please think about it, I really don't want to lose you! Who would get the brass so shinny if you leave? You're the only one to clean it the way you do." That was true. I ended up starting work half an hour early each morning just to clean the brass. It was so shinny when I had cleaned it, you could use it for a mirror. Even on my day off I would go and clean it, so I never ever got a lie in.

Barry had heard that I was leaving The Silver Fox and was up there faster than I could blink. "What's going on, Belinda?" he asked. "When are you going back to Scotland?"

"I'm not going back to Scotland, silly, I'm only leaving The Silver Fox."

He asked where I was going to live, and I told him that Alexandra had offered me a room.

"Oh, Thank God for that, I thought you were moving back to Scotland," he said. I think deep down Barry thought that one day I would succumb to him. Although I left The Silver Fox, I still went there once or twice a week for a drink and a sing along with Jeff and Dave. I was in there one Friday evening with Alexandra when Barry walked in with a couple of friends, so we all sat together and had a good old natter. It was such a funny night.

One of his friends, in particular, was a little over friendly but a lovely man, every time he spoke to me he had this glint in his eye and kept putting his hand on my leg when he was telling me a story. It was kind of funny though, because it was so noticeable that he fancied me. Barry noticed it too and didn't look best pleased about it although he didn't say anything. Alexandra and I went home that night happy that we had such a good night.

I woke up the next morning raring to go, got dressed, had breakfast, then I was out the door. Job hunting didn't prove too hard and I found a job that day, although it was only behind the bar in a pub in Bryn Deri in the evenings.

It was only a couple of days after that, that I found a job during the day as well. So that was me sorted; working ten until two, then home for a few hours before starting work in the pub from seven until closing time. *Fab* I thought, *I had everything sorted.*

Then, after a couple of weeks, I thought I should change my shifts. Eventually, I talked my day job into letting me work from nine until five, finishing at one on a Friday. My evening job changed to Friday, Saturday and Sunday. It was great I had my evenings free on Monday to Thursday and my days free Saturday and Sunday.

The pub in Bryn Deri was much bigger than The Silver Fox and was just up the road from the pub I went to on the day I arrived in Wales. So it was not a surprise when some of the locals knew who I was because they were in the pub on the day I arrived and took note of me being the newcomer.

I got to know a couple of the lads and we got on very well too. I didn't, however, get the same reception from many of the girls. That was no surprise though; I've always had this reaction, except for when I was young and I had a few female friends.

As I have got older it seems to be men who make better friends. A lot of woman don't really like me for some reason. They see me as some kind of a threat, or at least so I've been told, which is a great shame because I have so much to give, if only they would let their guard down.

I was pouring a drink one night when I looked across the room to see another familiar face; Barry's friend from that night out in The Silver Fox a couple of weeks back. He was sitting with some friends and I could tell he was talking about me because they all kept looking over. I was a little embarrassed and, I have to admit, seeing him again gave me a little tickle in my tummy. I don't know why, because I didn't feel as though I was attracted to him the last time I saw him. He came over after a little while and asked for a couple of drinks.

"Have a drink yourself, Belinda," he said.

"Thank you, Peter, but I'm not allowed to drink on duty, so I will put the money in the jar." "When did you start working here?" he asked.

"A couple of weeks ago," I replied, "and I love it." I told him about my job during the day and my reasons for leaving The Silver Fox.

"Do you live here now then?"

"No," I replied, "I live in Mawr with Alexandra."

"Small world," he said, "I live in there too."

"Alexandra is a nice girl," I added, "we get on well and go out from time to time for a drink; she works round the corner from here."

"Really? Well, maybe I will see you around the village now that we are neighbours."

"I hope so," I said. *Why the hell did I say that?* I thought to myself as Peter went back to sit with his friends, I don't really know him.

It was the way he looked at me, it did something to me. He had beautiful blue eyes, a lovely smile and blond hair. If he had had black hair, he would have looked a little like Sylvester Stallone.

I spent the next couple of weeks working away and doing my thing, I had several offers from some of the lads to go out on a date but I turned them all down. Who knows, maybe one of them may have been my soul mate!

Peter came into the pub most weekends after that initial encounter. I would hear one of the boys say to him. "Aye, you're in here more than you are at home these days, we only used to see you once every couple of months."

"It's the beer," he said, "since the new barmaid arrived, it seems to leave a pleasant taste in my mouth." I blushed, but felt good because I knew he was talking about me.

A couple of hours later Peter came over to me, "Belinda, how about I stay and share your taxi home tonight, would you mind?"

"No, of course not," I said, "that would be nice." All of a sudden I couldn't wait to finish my shift, I had butterflies in my tummy and the rest of the night we couldn't seem to keep our eyes of each other.

Peter said to the taxi driver, "Just here will do, thanks." It was the bus stop facing the house where I now lived.

"How did you know I lived here," I asked?

I live over there just past the pub. (I found out some time later why he really stopped at that bus stop.)

"I haven't been in that pub yet, I've been so busy working."

"Well, you will have to come in then, when you can, it's a cosy little pub and my local."

"Your local?" I said, "I thought the pub I worked in was your local because you're in there all the time."

"Ah," he replied, "that's only because you work there." Then he blushed.

"Well, I don't work on Saturday during the day so I will pop in tomorrow and see what the local pub is like."

"You do that, and I'll make sure I'm there too." There was a silence between us for what seemed like hours. "Can I kiss you Belinda?" he asked eventually. I looked at Peter but didn't know what I should say, my heart was pounding.

"Yes," I said. He took me in his arms and kissed me with such passion, I hadn't felt that feeling for years. In fact, I had never felt that feeling. He walked me to the front door and kissed me again, this time for longer and it was so gentle and passionate.

"Goodnight, Belinda, I'll see you tomorrow in the pub. I'll be in there around two o'clock." "Goodnight, Peter, and thank you."

"No," he said, "thank you."

6
A New Man in My Life

He was right, it was a lovely little pub, in fact it was also a bed and breakfast and the owners were nice too. What I loved about it was the coal fire and the cosiness. The people were friendly enough but again I was struck by that quietness, like, okay, I'm a newcomer what are you all looking at?

Peter came in but wasn't alone, Barry was with him. I could tell by the look on Barry's face that he wasn't pleased that Peter had come to meet me.

"Hi, I see you made it then, what do you think of my local?" Peter asked.

"I love it, very warm and friendly." Or so I thought, some of the locals just wouldn't stop staring. In fact, I would have said by the look on their faces that something was wrong. Peter went to the toilet and Barry leaned a little closer, chatting away, and then he said, "Belinda…"

"Yes, Barry what's up?" But just as he was about to tell me, Peter came back, so Barry moved away from me a little. I didn't want to pursue it because I felt that what he wanted to say was private. We all played pool for a while and had a good old laugh, but some of the locals still kept looking at me, from time to time, as if I had two heads.

After a while, Peter asked if he could meet me at the bus stop again that night when I finished work. I said, Yes, No hesitation. The rest of the afternoon was spent chatting and playing darts with Peter brushing against me every now and then, it made the hairs on my arms stand up with excitement. It made me feel like we were naughty kids trying to hide something, which made it all the more fascinating.

I left the pub that afternoon at five and from then until the time I finished work, seemed to drag, waiting for my meeting with Peter. When he arrived at the bus stop he didn't see me at first because it was so dark. He wasn't alone, he had his dog in tow.

"Aww, nice dog," I said.

"Sorry, Belinda but I had to walk him. How are you?"

"I'm good, thanks." He tied the dog to the shelter and took me in his arms, once again those feeling came flooding back. I was so excited I thought I would burst.

He said what I knew he would eventually say; that he felt something for me. I too had those feelings and was surprised because, although I had briefly dated a few men since moving to Wales, none of them had made me feel like that, until now. I lay in bed that night dreaming, just like us girls do, imagining Peter lying there beside me. He was so gentle and handsome.

Then it came to me like someone had thrown a book at me to get my attention. I hardly knew him, what was happening? Then I found myself crying and thinking about Leanne, my daughter, my little girl. I broke my heart that night as it all came flooding back. What was I going to do? I wanted my child so badly and I missed her so much that my heart ached. I was scared, broken and tried to fight my thoughts. I didn't want to think, I needed to sleep and wake up to a new day with no thoughts at all of my other life.

On Sunday morning, I was up with the birds, in the bath and dressed, then had breakfast. It was a cold day, and winter was fast approaching. I chopped logs for the fire, then set it all ready to light later. Alexandra didn't have central heating and it was the coal fire that heated the house so when it was cold it was really cold. I loved chopping the logs. In fact, I love coal fires. Maybe they remind me of my childhood sitting with a slice of bread at the end of a very long fork waiting to toast it before going to school. I decided to go for a walk over 'the tops'.

They were called 'the tops' because the path went over the hills, although they seemed like mountains to me. I walked for about an hour before I arrived in Ebbw Vale, a beautiful town on the other side of the hills, full of shops, restaurants and cafés. There was one café I found which became my haven and still is to this day. I go there whenever I go to Wales. It wasn't anything special inside but did have a wonderful book shop upstairs. I spent many hours in here over the years. I would also think of Barry as this was where he brought me on a night out and showed me around. It was a lovely place and Barry's company was something special because he was so kind, lovely, and an all-round genuine lad. It was such a shame I couldn't have the same feelings for him that he had for me.

The week passed and, before I knew it, it was Friday. I was serving pints when Peter came over to me. "I didn't even know you were here," I said.

"I just came in." He had a sad look on his face. "Belinda, I can't stay but can I meet you at the bus stop tonight?"

Yes, you okay?

"No, not really, my nain passed away a couple of days ago and the funeral was today." Nain was Welsh for gran.

"Oh, Peter, I'm so sorry to hear that. Yes, I will be there, what time?"

"Can we make it about twelve thirty?"

"Yes, but why so late?" I asked.

"I'll explain later, he said.

The rest of the night seemed to go so slowly and my concentration was just as bad, everyone was asking what was wrong with me. I told them I had a headache.

7
He's Married

I was standing at that bus stop, cold and tired, but I knew I had to wait even if Peter was late, he had really looked worried. Maybe, he was going to tell me that he didn't want to see me again. I could see Peter walking towards me looking down to the ground. He walked up to me put his arms around me and gently kissed me on the lips.

"What's wrong, Peter?"

"Is Alexandra home?" he enquired.

"No," I said she is staying over with her mum.

"Can I come into the house with you?"

"Yes, of course, come on, it's freezing."

The house was cosy and warm when we walked in; Alexandra had lit the coal fire before she left, as she normally did for me coming in from a cold night. I poured a drink for us both and we snuggled up next to the fire.

"What's wrong, Peter, why do you look so sad?" I asked.

"You know that we buried my nain today?"

"Yes," I said, "it must have been very hard for you and your family. I'm really sorry that you had to go through that, it's never easy to bury a loved one."

"I know. Its like I've had my heart ripped out of me. It's not easy, Belinda, and the only thing that got me through today was knowing that I could see you tonight."

"I'm here for you anytime, Peter, always remember that," I said.

Peter looked at me and said, "Belinda take me to bed." I was gobsmacked but at the same time very nervous. I hadn't slept with anyone in almost two years since I broke up with Michael, my daughter's father. We stood up, drinks in hand, and walked towards the stairs, now my heart was really pounding. All sorts of things were running through my mind. *Oh my God*, I thought, *what if I have forgot how to…*

I had only been with Michael; he was my first and only love. We met each other when I was in high school and had been together for eight years. Yes, I had had several boyfriends after that but there was no intimacy. Before I knew it my past was no longer on my mind. Peter kissed me with such passion but at the same time was gentle and caring.

I could feel every inch of my body tingle each time he caressed and kissed me, it was like nothing I had never felt before in my life. I didn't want it to end and, for the first time ever, I had lost all my inhibitions.

We kissed each other in places, I didn't know existed. I wanted him to take me right there and then but he didn't. He kept me waiting and he made me feel so special. After about half an hour, I couldn't wait any longer, the passion between us was incredible. I knew that, because he had got me so worked up with foreplay, I would burst with pleasure the minute he entered me.

I didn't and we made love in ways I had never before explored, and I enjoyed it. I could hear him moan with pleasure as did I. I played out those roles that we, as women, only imagine, that is, until we know we are with the right person. The feeling of wanting to be connected to his body and never leave was unbreakable and continued for a long time to come.

We lay there for another hour after we made love, then fell asleep, waking in the morning at eight thirty. He looked at me before taking me in his arms. "I will stay with you for a while if you don't mind," he said. Then Peter took me in his arms and again we made passionate love, I thought to myself, *where have you been all my life?*

I didn't know that making love could be so fantastic. It was at this point that I realised I was in love with Peter, and I *mean* 'in love'. I thought I was in love with Michael but came to understand that, although it was love… I wasn't 'in love'. The rest of the week I was in a day-dream and couldn't wait until my next shift at the pub just to see Peter again.

Although I walked around the village, I never saw him, and didn't even know what house he lived in. I bumped into Barry on my walk one day and it was good to see him. I hadn't seen him since that day in the pub in the village.

"Well, hello, stranger," he said, "how are you doing?"

"I'm good, thanks, how are you?"

"I've just finished work and am on my way to The Silver Fox. Come with me if you're stuck for something to do." As we walked along the road, we talked about the weather mostly and how cold it was. Barry told me that he had met a girl and he was thinking of proposing to her.

"That's great news, Barry, I'm very happy for you. You're a great guy and deserve someone special."

It was cosy in The Silver Fox, with the coal fire burning, and it kind of made me wish I was still working there. I missed it.

"Belinda, can I ask you something?" said Barry.

"Of course, what's up? What's the deal with you and Peter?"

"We have been seeing each other from time to time, although I haven't seen him this last week."

"Please don't think I'm interfering, Belinda. Peter is a sound mate and you are also a good friend, but did you know that he is married?"

"MARRIED! Are you serious? No, I didn't." To be truthful, I hadn't even given a thought as to whether he was with someone or not; I was so wrapped up in him. What on earth was I thinking? Barry could see the disappointment in my face.

"I thought not, but I think it's right that you should know, I can see that you have fallen for Peter."

"Oh no, Barry, what am I going to do? You're right; I have fallen for him, although I wondered if he has changed his mind because I haven't seen him in a week now."

"Belinda, I just wanted you to know, because I don't want to see you hurt and, really, Peter should have told you before now."

"I'm glad that you told me, Barry. I can decide now what I should do next."

8
Lies and Reservations

Here I was with a dilemma on my hands, what on earth was I going to do? The thought of being with a man who was married suckered me, yet I had completely fallen for him.

Another week went by before I saw Peter again. I was pouring a pint for a young lad when he walked up and waited to be served.

"Well, hello, stranger," I said, trying to hide my disappointment at not seeing him since our night together.

"How are you, Belinda?"

"I'm fine, thanks, what about you? I haven't seen you for a while and thought maybe I had scared you off."

"There's no chance of that happening. I would like to see you tonight, though we have to talk."

"Okay," I said.

So that was it for the next couple of hours, and I wondered if he was going to tell me about his wife. Arriving back at the house, I thought to myself, *well, no making love tonight, no way, how dare he not tell me about his wife*. When he arrived, I couldn't wait for him to get to the point so I did it for him.

"Peter, why didn't you tell me you were married? I had to find out from someone else."

"Belinda, please listen, I am married but I have been separated from my wife for some time now. Well, actually I'm not going to lie; my wife and I have been having problems for a few years. Do you remember the night I came to you?"

The night you buried your nain? Yes, I do.

"Well, that was the final straw for me and my wife, she has never been there when I needed her and it hurts, so the day of the funeral, she started her usual whining and I couldn't take it anymore. I knew she wouldn't want to listen to me and how I felt about that day. After you and I spent the night together, I decided that was it and I moved out the next day."

"I see, and do you have children?"

"Yes, I have two daughters who are my world. I see them every day and will have them a couple of nights each week. I'm staying with my parents right next to the pub and garage, so it's not far from there to my other house."

"Peter, can you promise me that I didn't have any part in your decision to leave your wife and children? I won't be a part of a relationship breakup, no way, that's not me."

"I promise it has nothing to do with you." I kind of felt a little relieved, although I still didn't believe he was being one hundred percent truthful.

Those feelings soon disappeared after he asked me to hold him. I did feel bad about doubting him but then I knew that I had fallen in love with him. I took him in my arms and we kissed, that kiss seemed to last forever and I had butterflies in my stomach. Goosebumps came all over me as he stroked my neck and slowly, very slowly, let his hand move around until he touched my breasts. At that moment I felt like I was about to explode. *How could a man make a woman feel that good?* I asked myself, as he unbuttoned my blouse and his fingers caressed me to the point that I wanted him to take me right then.

I have to admit the build-up to it was so beautiful and when we did make love it lasted such a long time. Afterwards, we would just lie there in each other's arms until the feeling started all over again, and when we kissed the passion was ecstatic; he made me feel like we could be locked together forever.

Needless to say, I wasn't a very popular girl in that village because it soon got round that Peter was with another woman, something they had suspected from the first day I entered that pub which explained why it was so quiet and why everyone kept staring. Yip that woman from Scotland. Boy did they make me feel bad with their glares of disapproval.

That night my thoughts turned, once again, to my daughter, Leanne, and for some unknown reason, Michael. Although we were no longer together, I did feel a little like I was betraying him. Why, I don't know, but what I did realise was that I could not keep shutting Leanne out of my thoughts. I longed so badly for her and I knew that if I went back to Scotland I would end up back with her father because, deep down, I still loved him.

Maybe I believed that, if I went back, we could be a family again and if I tried hard enough we could make it work for our daughter, but I also thought if I returned and it didn't work out, I would stay anyway because it was the only way we could be together.

As the months went on, I worked, I went out and I had fun but I was still drinking to block out the things I knew that soon I must face up to. Why did I find it so hard to stand my ground? And the sad thing was, the longer I left it, the harder it became. I would call Leanne every weekend and we would chat for some time and not once would her father talk to me. At the end of every call I ended up in tears.

I decided to leave my pub job in Bryn Deri and went to work in the Cambrian in Ebbw Vale, a small, cosy, little pub run by an Irish man called Ben. I loved my job at the Cambrian. Ben made me feel so welcome and always had some sandwiches and a cup of tea on a tray for me before I started work.

"Come into the sitting room," he would say, in that fine Irish accent. "You sit here eat and keep warm. Now, pretty blue eyes," as he would call me, "tell me about your day!"

I used to ask him to tell me stories about Ireland and he very kindly would chat away for a while. It was only a matter days before some of the locals from the pub in Bryn Deri turned up after hearing that I worked there and they then made it a regular occurrence to come for a drink and a chat, much to the annoyance of Peter.

He didn't like me having attention from other men which, at first, I found quite endearing until eventually it got out of hand.

A couple of months later, Peter took me out for a quiet drink and we chatted away about all the usual stuff, but by this time I was getting a little fed up with having to hide at the back of pubs so that we wouldn't offend any of the locals from the village, as they still did not approve of us being a couple. To them, I was Peter's mistress and responsible for the break-up of his marriage.

I said to Peter, "I can't take this anymore, why don't you stand up for yourself and tell people the truth? Or was that just what you told me so I wouldn't end our relationship?"

Again, Peter assured me that it was nothing to do with me. What could I do? In one hand I wanted to end it because I felt for his wife, even though Peter promised me it was over before I came along, but on the other hand I loved him. I wanted to be with him, I wanted him so badly.

"Belinda," he said, "I have something I need to ask you!"

"What's wrong," I asked? Apparently, there was a rumour going around the village that Paulo and a couple of his friends had said they had slept with me and now the whole Mawr village was talking about it. Peter asked me if it was true.

"WHAT!" I shouted. "Are you serious, and you have to ask me if this is true? Well, it's obvious you don't know me well enough, if you have to ask. The answer is most definitely NO." I stood up, said goodbye and walked out of the door.

I didn't see Peter again for a couple of weeks after that. I was furious, I didn't realise until later that I should have stayed and faced those idiots. Paulo and his Friends were women mad and would sleep with anything that had legs, except me, because I have respect for myself and wouldn't have touched any of them.

Another week went by before Peter came knocking at the door. He just stood there looking at me, before finally saying he was sorry. I asked him why? Why had he chosen to believe stupid stories? He said that he didn't want to believe them but had to be sure. He also said that he had been lonely and upset not seeing me, and then he said, "I love you."

I knew I also loved him but I wanted to make him suffer. I was still outraged by the fact that this story was circulating around the village. We had arranged to see one another again in the local pub, but I told Peter we would sit like a couple and not hide round the back, and if he felt he couldn't do that, then I didn't want to see him again.

I could see the look of shock on his face and, although I didn't really mean it, I wanted to show him that I was no pushover. The next day, I walked along to the pub and did something I had never done before; I walked into the pub on my own and I held my head high. Everything and everybody stopped. You could have heard a pin drop and I was shaking like a leaf but was determined not to let these people get the better of me. The barmaid said to me, "The usual, Belinda?"

"Yes, please, Janet," I replied, and stood there like nothing was wrong. No sooner than she had served my drink, the door opened. It was Peter and now everybody stood there waiting to see what was going to happen next.

He walked over to me and kissed my cheek. I was stunned, I was so proud of him for doing that, but the local's looked on with that disappointed look on their faces.

About an hour after we had settled down with our drink the door opened and who do you think walked in? *Well, Well, Well,* I thought, *perfect. Now the shit really is going to hit the fan.* I waited and I observed while Paulo and his friends got their drinks and settled into the usual routine and then, just when they thought everything was hunky dory, I walked over to the bar.

I looked at them and said, "Can I just ask you to tell everybody when I slept with each of you and how was it? Was I good?" The whole pub was silent and then Paulo and his friends started to laugh.

"Oh, Belinda," said Paulo, "you know that was just some fun."

"Oh, really," I said, "so I didn't sleep with you?"

"No, no, Belinda, it was just a joke."

"Really? Well, from this moment on, you keep your bloody jokes to yourself. And now that I have cleared that up," I addressed the rest of the pub, "maybe you lot can stop judging me and try to get to know me."

Instead of everyone chatting, some sat in silence and some were whispering but Paulo and his friends were so embarrassed they ended up walking out, all except one that is. He just continued drinking and chatting like nothing had happened.

Peter had booked a table for the following weekend in that same pub and, much to my surprise, people actually started to talk to me. Well, some did, others took a little longer to come round. Peter's wife had decided some weeks before to move away; not too far, but drivable for Peter to pick up his children for weekends.

I must admit, even though I still felt bad over the whole situation, I did feel some kind of relief when she moved. I think it helped some of the locals to speak to me without feeling bad. Even Peter's parents started talking more.

9
Missing My Daughter

About a month later, Peter and I were in the pub having a meal, and out of nowhere he got down on his knee and brought this small box out of his pocket. I was so shocked because the room was full of diners, and then he said, "Belinda will you marry me?"

I didn't know where to look; I was so embarrassed but people were looking at me, as if waiting to hear my answer. After a minute or so, I said, "Yes." I surprised myself because I didn't really have time to think about it. If it hadn't been for that room full of people I would have said I needed time to think.

It seemed such a sham too, being that he wasn't even divorced yet, but what could I do? I didn't want to turn him down in front of all those people and make him feel bad. Before I knew it half the village knew about our engagement and a couple of days later I went to the local shop and they congratulated me. I said, "Thank you, boy news travels fast."

The next few weeks seemed like a blur but, in reality, it was anything but, on my mind now was, do I want to marry Peter or not? Do I want to continue with this new life in Wales or do I go home and sort things out with my child's father so that my daughter is in my life again?

I knew the answer and Leanne won hands down. I was prepared to give up a life with a man I truly loved even though I had doubts after the rumour situation, but I kept quiet for now and decided I was going back to Scotland for a break to gather my thoughts and try to sort out things in respect of my daughter. I told Peter I was going back to Scotland for a few days and would be back before he knew it. Maybe this would give him time to see if this was what he really wanted too.

It was my first visit to Scotland since I arrived in Wales and I was really excited to see my family, but more excited to see my little girl. The first thing I did the day after I arrived was to phone Leanne and arrange to go and visit her and her father at her grandmother's house.

I was full of emotion and cried as soon as I saw her, I held her so tight I didn't want to let go and seeing Michael again made me wonder if I was doing the right thing in Wales? Michael went out for a while to give us some quality time. Her grandmother was also happy to see me, but did, in fact, want to talk to me privately as well. I wasn't prepared for what came next.

"Belinda," she said, "are you staying or going back?" I said that I didn't know and that I was confused. I needed to know that I could have Leanne back and, as long as that worked out, then, yes, I was staying. She told me that after my break-up with Michael, they had to call the Priest in to talk to him, and she said that when I left he sat for days rocking back and forth with my photo in his hand. She also said that Leanne would always ask, 'where is Mum? When is she coming back?' Although my little girl wondered where I was, she was only four and a half and most of the time thought I was away working, well that's what her grandmother said they told her.

I wanted to cry, hearing this made me feel terrible but at the same time I thought, *why am I being made to feel like this is my entire fault?* He was the one who betrayed me, he was the one who got drunk on a bottle of vodka and smashed the house up with an axe, he was the one who hit me and tried to whack me while holding our daughter. That night he was a madman, I was not going to be bullied anymore.

I remember the first time he hit me, I cowered in the corner like a small child, feeling humiliated as flashes of my childhood came rushing back. I had had so many hidings from my parents that when he hit me I thought it was normal, I was fed up with his drinking his gambling and the many times he would come home with either very little left of his wages or none at all.

Then there were the times he fought with his brother over some woman... How long did I have to put up with it? The funny thing was, I did still love him, he was my first love and the father of our child. He was tall, dark and extremely handsome and people said he looked like a rugby player. Many people thought he was older than me when, in fact, he was only one year older.

I used to be so proud, walking down the street with Michael hand in hand and, in all fairness, he would not let anyone take me for a mug. I was so jealous if I saw him talk to other woman (laughing my head of here, when I think of how the tables turned after Peter and I got engaged).

Michael made me feel special, and it's with fond memories even now when I think of how we started dating. He used to ride a motorbike and looked good on it. His aunt lived across the way from my parents and whenever he used to visit her I would have my eye on him. From the first time I saw him, I was in love. I used to think that I had no chance with a strapping handsome man and he wouldn't be seen with a scrawny little thing like me.

How wrong was I? His little cousin used to chat to me if he saw me outside and he would say, "My big cousin fancies you!"

I would be like, "Really, well I like him too," whilst blushing. This went on for some weeks and one day I asked him, "What sort of music does your big cousin like?"

"Adam and the Ants," he replied.

"Wow," I said, "so do I, my favourite song is 'Dog Eat Dog'." (I remember my friend and I used to dress like Adam Ant and we knew everything about him.)

Then he said, "He has that record."

"Well, maybe I should ask if I can borrow it."

"I'll ask him for you," he said. Boy, was I glad he said that, because I had no intention of asking him myself; I was a shy little thing.

A couple of days later, I was leaving my house to go to the shop when Michael was walking towards me. I felt my knees about to buckle below me.

"Belinda," he said, "I hear you like 'Dog Eat Dog'

"Yes, I do."

"Here is my copy if you want to listen to it. Just give me it back when your ready." I promised to return it the next time he was at his aunt's and he invited me over the following Friday. Well, that was me on a high. I couldn't believe he had taken the time to talk to me, let alone lend me his record. I was only fourteen then and he was fifteen. Prior to this I had only ever kissed two boys, and one of them kissed like a fish so I dumped him.

When I saw him on the Friday, we chatted for a bit and he asked me what school I went to and how old I was, all the usual stuff. Then he asked if I wanted to go for a ride on the back of his bike.

"I have a spare helmet," he said.

"Okay," I agreed eagerly, But I'll meet you at the top of the street because if my dad sees me, he will not be best pleased.

The ride on the back of that bike became a regular thing until one day we kissed and BAM! That was it, we started dating. I have to say though, he was such a lovable man, I couldn't wait to see him every time, I really did love him.

We did, over the years, have our little tiffs and fall out but nothing serious and we would only be away from each other at most a day before we had made up again. It's funny the way things turn out; we started dating on 29 July and two years later, on that same date, we got engaged, then after another two years on the same date our daughter was born. It was the proudest moment of our lives, more so mine; here I was almost nineteen and I had my own home. Nobody could boss me around or hit me anymore, at least that's what I thought, until Michael hit me for the first time.

Even today I have a lot of respect for Michael. Although we were fourteen and fifteen when we started dating he didn't pressure me to go any further than a kiss. I was seventeen before I lost my virginity.

I told his grandmother that I still loved him but could not live the way we had lived before; with the lies and the deceit, not to mention the possibility that he went behind my back with another woman. Don't get me wrong, I was no angel but I was not a bad person and would never have gone with another man while I was with him.

I did, however, have plenty of opportunity. One man even asked me to leave Michael while I was pregnant. He said he wanted me, even though I was having another man's child. I turned him down of course because that's not me. That same man and I are still good friends to this day we have known each other for many years.

Michael was told by his sister-in-law that she had seen me kiss another man while I was at work, untrue of course. The result was him drinking a bottle of vodka and trying to beat me. No more, was I going to be at the end of a man's fist nor have my daughter around that behaviour either.

I remember one occasion, when he came home from work he had been to the pub and had a few drinks, we rowed that night and he kicked me on the leg with his steel toe cap boots which resulted in my leg bleeding. Leanne was just under two-years-old and she started crying saying to her dad, "Don't hit Mum." That broke my heart and from then on things continued to go downhill.

Sometime later, my daughter's dad returned and it was time for me to go. I asked him if he would give me a lift home. He said yes and, at this point, we were just on talking terms. When we got to the car park outside my parents we sat and talked for a while.

He said that he still loved me and I told him the same. I wanted to ask him if things would change if I came back, but I was afraid to, so I kept quiet. He also told me that he had met someone and was happy. I felt quite gutted. He also told me that he was granted full custody of our daughter; then I saw red.

"What! How could that be possible? I said, "I thought it was going to court?"

"It did, but you didn't turn up."

"What do you mean? I wasn't told of any court date?" He said that a letter had been sent to my parents' house. I told him that I would speak to them and get back to him but not before letting him know I was furious.

When I spoke to my parents about this they said they had never received a letter for me for court. I believed them, until I found out later that, in fact, they had and they even signed for it. They just failed to tell me because they did not want me to come back and bring any trouble.

It was typical of my parents, as they hadn't given me support when I lost my daughter anyway. I knew then I was fighting a losing battle and by this time Leanne had already been in school a couple of years; it would have been selfish of me to try and take her away now. I decided to leave things as they were but to see my solicitor to apply for access throughout the year.

I was already calling her every weekend and every time I came home to Scotland I would have her stay with me. As much as all this broke my heart and tore me in two I made up my mind to go back to Wales and marry Peter.

10
Jealously and Suspicion

The trip back to Wales gave me a lot of time to think. Michael and I had had words and stopped speaking again which broke my heart because, if there is one thing I didn't want, that was to lose contact or the love I still had for him.

Many things went through my mind that day and one of them was to stop blaming myself for everything that had happened and to face up to the fact that I had lost Leanne now and to carry on trying for access to her. I hadn't, by this stage, told Peter that I had a daughter but knew that if we were to marry I needed to be upfront and tell him everything. Well, maybe not everything, but definitely about Leanne and the fact that I would be trying either to get full custody or part access on school holidays throughout the year.

Peter actually took it better than I thought. He also told me, while we were being honest, that he wanted me to stop working in pubs. I asked if there was any particular reason why.

"I don't like other men being over friendly with you," he said. I agreed to give in my notice, just like that. What on earth was I thinking?

A part of me found it very endearing that Peter didn't like the attention I got and it showed me that he really did love me, even though I knew deep down I enjoyed working the pubs. so I handed in my notice. It wasn't until about a year later, I realised just how bad Peter's obsession about me not being around other men had become. It wasn't just a jealous thing, it was possession, and boy did that have some serious consequences.

As I walked through the village one day I was met by Jeff, who sang in the pubs, and I asked him how he was. I wasn't ready for what he said next.

"Belinda, I can't talk to you. I'm sorry!"

"What? What do you mean, you can't talk to me? Have I upset you?"

"No, not at all, it's that man you're seeing..." Jeff hadn't really known Peter until recently.

"Peter? What about him?"

"I was going into the pub for a drink last week and, as he was leaving, he said he wanted a word with me... He told me that the pub was his local and I was not welcome there."

"Why would he tell you that?"

I don't know, but he said that if he ever saw me talking to you he would 'sort me out'.

"Oh, he did, did he? Well, don't mind him, I will have a word."

When I asked Peter what was going on he said that he did not want Jeff to talk to me as he knew that we had dated. That's when I knew his jealousy was just a tad strange. Still, I didn't care to take it further, I had no energy to. Peter's divorce had come through and he didn't leave it too long before setting a date to get married.

On 6 April 1991, we were at the Registry Office waiting to say, 'I do' that date was also the anniversary of his friend and his wife, so it was kind of a double celebration. Barry was at the wedding too, and he said to me on the quiet that Peter was a very lucky man and kissed my cheek. That was a lovely thing for him to say considering we dating briefly. I still felt kind of bad because if, I had been ready at that time, it may have been he and I that were getting married.

My family came down from Scotland and, I have to say, some had mixed emotions about the family I was marrying into. Don't get me wrong, they loved Peter, but they felt a slight hint of disapproval from some of his family. I learned why years later, and they were right. Peter's father was the one who disapproved the most; for some reason or another he just didn't want Peter to marry me. I'm not sure if it was because I was Scottish or something else, but he did make a remark to my aunt which she said confirmed that he didn't want us to get married. To this day she hasn't told me what he said.

The first year of our marriage was wonderful. We were both very much in love and the passion between us and intimacy was like nothing on earth, well, actually, the earth moved every time! I had never experienced anything like it and I gave so much, so much in fact that Peter later said to me that he had never been with any woman who made him feel as wonderful or who made love with such passion.

We did a lot together and I loved living in Mawr. After we got engaged I moved out of Alexandra's house and in with Peter's sister, where I stayed for around three, maybe four, months until we got our own home. I used to love going up the hills with the chainsaw and sawing logs for the coal fire. I could go to work in my suit by day and be wearing jeans to chop logs by night.

Soon after we married, I found a new full time job in a factory dealing with medical records from which I ended up with a manager's position. It was here that I met my close friends from Bryn Deri and we became more like family. I loved them all, as they were there for me from the first day I met them, one in particular I'm still close to this day. My friend, Ruth, and her husband are such wonderful parents; they have four children and I have watched them grow from young children to beautiful adults with lovely children of their own. She also has a sister and three brothers, one of which I am very fond of and very close too. In fact, after Peter and I split up we could have been a couple because there was always an attraction there and I still love him to bits to this day, but he was already taken back then and we both knew that it could not be.

Around a year after the wedding, I spoke to Peter about having children which is something we had discussed before we got married but, all of a sudden, he decided that he didn't want to have more children. So I thought I would leave it a little longer before approaching the subject again.

Then one day I was sitting in the kitchen and out of nowhere he said to me, "I don't want more kids."

I said, "Of course you do, you said before we married that you would have another child."

"No, Belinda I really don't want to and if you do, then we can't be together anymore."

I was dumbfounded. "Are you saying that you want to end our marriage?"

"No," he said, "I don't, but if you want children then you need to think about it."

I was confused, "Peter, I said to you a couple of months ago that it was almost time for me to stop taking the pill because of my age, and if we wanted to have more children it would need to be soon."

"I don't want any more and that's it, if you want to come off the pill then you need to get sterilised or our marriage is over."

All I could do was leave the room and go upstairs to try and make sense of what he had said. I cried my eyes out. *That's it,* I thought. My only child was almost 300 miles away and I ached for her so badly, I had two step-daughters whom I loved, but only saw every fortnight, and now, no more kids! *What the hell was I going to do?*

Although we hadn't fallen out, conversation between us was a little frosty to say the least, and for days I went around as if on another planet. Then the time came to sit down and have it out with him once and for all.

I said to him, "Peter, I love you very much and if you are absolutely sure that you don't want more kids, then why don't you go and have the operation?"

Why Me?

"Because it's you who does not want them. If anything happens to you and I were to meet someone else, he may want kids."

"So, what are you saying? You may find another man…" He had such a horrid look on his face.

"No, that's not what I'm saying, but it's only fair that you get it done because it's you who does not want any more children."

"Well," he said, "then it looks like we may have to get a divorce, because I won't have the operation."

After a couple of days, I ended up giving in and I arranged to have it done but deep down I knew I was making a huge mistake. What was I to do? I was in love with Peter and wanted to spend the rest of my life with him.

I told him that I would always resent him for making me to go through with it. He didn't much like it but he knew he too loved me and didn't want to lose me, but it still didn't make him change his mind.

The day of the operation approached and he couldn't even take me to the hospital, it was his mother who took me. I can't even remember our conversation in the car that day because my mind was elsewhere. I hoped that I would be in hospital and just before the operation he would appear and tell me not to do it, but he didn't.

After the operation, I was in hospital for four days and they told me when I left that I had to have two weeks' rest before going back to work. *Two weeks,* I thought, *no way, a couple of days will do me.*

After the first week I decided to go back to work. I was really bored sat at home all day, every day. I wasn't in work long before I passed out and was taken home again. I wasn't well for some time after that as the bleeding just didn't seem to stop and it was accompanied by a lot of pain.

When I eventually returned to work, it was a little easier but I still didn't feel great, so I went to the doctor to see what was wrong. They took some blood tests and sent me home, but things weren't right and I was still bleeding.

11
A Gun to My Head

I will never forget the phone call that I received at work shortly after. The doctor called and said, "It's possible that you were pregnant when we sterilised you."

"WHAT!" I dropped the phone, tears running down my face. My boss, Pam, also now one of my closest friends, took the phone from me and asked what was going on. I cannot begin to tell you what a bolt it was to hear those words, and from that moment the resentment for my husband set in big time. All I could think was, *you bastard, how you could put me through all this?*

Thinking back now, maybe it was meant to be, as another child would not, and could not, replace my daughter. Nor did I want it that way.

It took a few months for us to get back to normal but it was never the same as it was before, although I think Peter thought it was, and carried on as if nothing had happened.

One day, I was doing my hair getting ready for work and he said to me, "I wish you could go to work with a bag over your head."

"What on earth makes you say a thing like that?" I asked.

"I hate other men looking at you."

"You know, Peter, this has to stop," I said. "If someone in the village tells you they've seen me talking to a man, you're on my back. Who is he? How do you know him? What were you talking about? I'm sick of it, get over yourself, I married you because I love you not because I want to chat up other men."

To make matters worse, he spotted Jeff again, coming out of the pub. With rage in his eyes, he said to him, "You have one week to leave this village and go back to where you came from or I will shoot you."

I seriously don't know what possessed him to say such a thing but I was beginning to wonder if there was something wrong in his head. During one of my driving lessons the instructor had leaned behind his seat to get his folder and, while doing so, I saw Peter over the other side of the car park walking towards the car with something in his hand. Next thing he turned round and went back into our car.

When I left the instructor and got into our car I asked him what he had been doing, he said, "I thought he was making a pass at you, so I was going to smack him." When I looked down Peter had a meat clever in his hand.

That was the last straw for me (always the last straw!). I told him I was going to tell his dad. He begged me not to, and said it wouldn't happen again.

It was time for another trip home to Scotland and, this time, Peter came with me, but he never did again after that. He told me he hated Scotland but the truth of the matter was that that was where my past was, my daughter and her father, and that was why he didn't want to go back.

After that, I always went to Scotland on my own. I would travel up every three to five months but that last year was more frequent. It was during one summer holiday I said to Peter, "I'm going to go home for a week this time, I need to spend a little more time with Leanne."

Well, you would have thought I threw a rag to a bull, he was like a madman, gun in hand, as he was ready to go rabbit hunting. He lifted that gun right in front of my face, loaded, which it shouldn't have been until he was up the tops. He started to shout at me, "That's right, you go back to Scotland, back to your daughter and your ex and leave me here again."

I was shocked, and told him that he was welcome to come, but that he had said he hated Scotland. He just wouldn't listen and his rage got worse. I was afraid of what he might do next and I don't know where I got the strength from, but I grabbed the gun away and before I knew it, he had punched me in the face.

I burst into tears, and it was like someone switched on a light as he realised what he had done.

"Oh my God, Belinda," he said, "I'm so sorry, I don't know what came over me, please, I have never hit a woman before."

I told him, "If you ever do that to me again, I will make sure when the police come to review your gun licence renewal, that you won't get it, and I'm telling your father." He begged me not to and swore it would never happen again. Something I have heard all too often; that he wouldn't do it again.

I didn't tell his dad but I should have, I knew if I told him he would have sorted Peter out big time. His father was a very strong-minded man and not someone you want to get on the wrong side of that's for sure. He was of the old school; no swearing in front of woman and behaving properly towards them. I think after that episode, Peter began to realise what he was doing and that he was in the wrong most of the time.

He had to change or I was out of there and things were better for a while but my health started to deteriorate. I lost weight; I was ten and half stone and kept going down, ten stone, nine and a half stone... I went to the doctor for a blood test after every weight loss but they couldn't find anything wrong.

I was very sleepy all the time and was losing my hair. I would have bouts of panic attacks and my weight eventually went down to seven and half stone. By this time I was really scared because I thought maybe I had cancer. Peter's aunt was dying from cancer and was so thin, of course I thought maybe that's what's wrong with me.

Eventually, I saw a student doctor and told me that for the last year I had had an overactive thyroid. He explained the results from a previous blood test, the year before, but was livid because my own doctor failed to spot the problem and get me on medication. If that doctor had not have spotted this I perhaps would not be here today.

Things were very cold and frosty between Peter and I. We didn't seem to get close anymore and he wasn't looking for it either, which I didn't understand, because if It was the time of the month and we couldn't be close, you could tell by his face that he was angry and the veins in his neck would stick out in frustration.

Looking back, he had to have sex all the time so there was obviously a problem there. I soon realised that all the weight loss made me unattractive to him as he liked his woman to be a little on the plump side, so to speak.

I didn't understand at the time, but realised later, the reason why he was starting work an hour earlier each morning, and no sooner had he been home and had his dinner he would be out again shooting or at his friend's.

I was back in Scotland close to Christmas and everyone was worried about the way I looked. They thought it was more than just an overactive thyroid, and I had to explain to them that things weren't so good down in Wales, but not to worry as it would come right. I had to say that, so as not to worry them, although, deep down, I knew that they realised there was more to it.

Michael and I had kind of patched things up and were on speaking terms again and, after another visit to his grandmother's, I got him to give me a lift home. It was then that we talked more openly about the past and we got to say a lot of things to each other that we hadn't back then but this time without falling out.

The funny thing was that he was with someone else now but she was eight years his junior. Boy, I didn't think that would have an impact on my feelings, but it did. He said that he had never stopped loving me and had told his new girl that he will always hold a place in his heart for me.

"That's lovely to hear," I said, "but it's a big mistake to say that to your new girlfriend." I told him that I still loved him too and that a couple of years previously, when he had taken me home, I had wanted to tell him so, but decided not to.

"I wish you had," he replied, "because then, we might have got back together."

"Well, it's a bit late now," I said, "and, besides, you love someone else." He told me that he didn't love her, and I asked why he had got engaged?

"Who else would have me, a grown man living with his grandmother and a child?" I told him he was crazy and couldn't mislead his girlfriend, and besides, he would find someone special eventually.

"Not like you," he said. "I don't love her, but I do care for her and maybe in time that will change."

I told him that whatever happened I would speak to him on Christmas Day and wished him well. I won't forget how, when he did come on the phone, he was very dry and abrupt with me. When I asked him, months later, why he had spoken to me the way he did, he said that his girlfriend did not want him to speak to me, unless it was important and about our daughter. I was furious but at the same time, I understood why. He should never have told her that he would always have a place in his heart for me.

12

The Great Pretender

Peter and I had holidays in some lovely countries, although he would never have gone overseas if he and I were not together. I was not about to do without my holidays abroad because he didn't like leaving Wales. I remember one particular holiday we went to Halkidiki in Greece, it was absolutely beautiful and the people where so friendly and welcoming.

We were out one night sitting by the bar, chatting to the barman; he was lovely and told us about all the local history. Shortly after, some of the staff came round for poolside drinks and a dance. This was in the early hours of the morning. I remember one of them asking me to join them in a traditional Greek dance, Zorba, and I jumped at the chance because I knew how to do it and loved it. Peter joined in after a short while but I could see he wasn't really enjoying the dancing.

However, I was having a great time and was not going to let him drag me away. We had worked and saved for this childfree holiday, so I wanted us to enjoy ourselves. It was around four thirty in the morning when everything started to wrap up and we all went to our apartments, Peter was very quiet and seemed a little odd.

When we were behind closed doors he pounced on me on top of the bed with his hands around my throat (it was not the first time he done this).

"What the hell are you doing?" I tried to shout.

"You were enjoying the attention from the barman and then he was dancing with you and you loved it." After a short struggle I managed to get out of his grip and jumped off the bed. "What the bloody hell are you talking about, you fucking freak?"

By this time I was a little drunk, because I wouldn't normally call someone names.

"Who are you calling a 'fucking freak'," he said, "You were the one dancing with the barman and you know he fancies you."

"I can't take this anymore, Peter, you are a fucking, crazy ass, Welsh twat." *Oh dear*, I thought, *things must be bad when I am shouting like this*. The whole of that area could hear us, although I didn't know that until the next day when the barman told me. On and on went Peter; he was so convinced that the barman and I had something going on.

The next morning we sat down to breakfast and I said to him, "Peter, I don't know what you thought was happening last night or what got into you but I was dancing with all those people, not just the barman, and if he fancied me as you say, then so what, as long as I'm not giving him the come on you have nothing to worry about.

"Do you think for one minute that I would be interested in some bloke who probably has it away with every woman who comes here on holiday? Let me tell you this, and understand what I am saying; if you ever touch me in that way again, or any other, with your hands or fists, and if you don't stop telling me who I can, and can't, talk to, then it is over. I mean it." He just sat there and didn't speak much for the next half hour. Eventually, when he did speak he said that he was sorry.

"I was so wound up last night," he explained, "I was embarrassed about dancing and when I saw how freely you got up to dance and hold their hands I saw red, I suppose the drink didn't help either."

"Peter," I said, do you think that dancing to Zorba can be done without touching hands? It can't, that's how it's done. Please, you really do have to stop this. You're making me feel ill and sick. You have a problem and you need to get it sorted out. It's one thing to be a little jealous that's normal... but you are possessive and that's not healthy.

"You will push me away if you keep doing this. Go and see a doctor because you know it's that bad. Were you like this with your ex-wife? Probably not, but then Peter she didn't go anywhere, did she? She didn't work and was at home with the kids all the while so she didn't get the chance to talk to men or anyone for that matter."

"Belinda, I just hate the thought of you not being with me and any other man having you. I hate the thought of you making love to another man the way you make love to me. I can't help it, maybe I do need help. If I ever thought you went with another man or that you would leave me I would throw acid over your face and then nobody could have you."

It was at that point I came to realise that Peter could be a dangerous man, I never did get that remark out of my mind.

For the next few months I was more or less in a daze. I went to work as usual but I just wasn't the same old me and it was noticed by everyone. No matter how often I would try to put on a smile, they knew it was false. Pam and I sat one day on our lunch break and she said to me, "I know things haven't been good of late with you and Peter, but it seems to be affecting you as a whole, you're not the same fun loving, bouncy Belinda anymore, do you want to talk?"

I remember a song came on the radio right then, it was Freddie Mercury's 'The Great Pretender'. My friend said to me, "This song reminds me of you." For a long time I wondered why, until I listened to the words and realised that she was right.

"Yes," I said, then I started to cry. "I don't know what's going on, things haven't been right for some months now. Peter isn't the same man I married. Don't get me wrong, I still love him very much but he is wearing me down with this possessive attitude of his."

Peter very often came and picked me up from work because I didn't drive and he would come in and have a chat with a couple of the girls because he knew them, and to everyone else he was just the same old Peter, although I knew differently. Lately, there had been disagreements and arguments here and there, and I knew that we had to sit down and get to the bottom of the problem or our marriage wasn't going to last much longer. It seemed that he was still plodding along doing his thing while I was being the dutiful wife.

We had had such fun over the years and done a lot together until that last year, when we stopped going out together unless we had an invite to visit his friends, and that's exactly what they were 'his friends'.

I got on well enough with them, they were really nice people but they weren't my people. I did start to wonder if they would ever be my people. One of the things I learned after we got married, the Welsh love the Scots but when you move into their territory it's a different story. I guess deep down I knew this from the day of the wedding but I was too wrapped up in everything to have noticed it. One thing is for sure, I came to understand years later that Peter's father wasn't keen on him having a baby with me. He didn't want a grandchild with Scottish blood, just like he didn't want his son to marry me. I've never understood why he felt this way. Maybe it's an old Welsh thing to stick to your own; I really don't know.

I remember the conversation like it was yesterday, I was in the kitchen having a bite to eat when Peter came through from the other room. "I want a divorce," he said. I thought I had heard wrong and kind of laughed. Thinking back what a fool I was.

"What did you just say?"

"I want a divorce," he repeated.

"Why?"

"I can't live like this anymore."

"So, clearly there is a problem, maybe we should discuss it," I said.

"You will always resent me for making you have that operation, you just won't forgive me for making you go through with it."

"You're damn right I won't forgive you and yes, I will always resent you for it. I told you this right up until that day but that doesn't mean I love you any less. I'm still very much in love with you, so why would you want a divorce? Have you stopped loving me? Because this last few months you have been different, we don't spend as much time together and you're always either working or out."

I have to admit that having a problem with my thyroid and the weight loss and panic attacks had probably made me a little unbearable at times, but what could I do? I also noticed that because I had lost so much weight, I lost my shape, my breasts were very small too and I must have looked terrible to Peter. Maybe I put him off? I did touch on the subject briefly, with him before and he admitted that he liked his woman to have some meat on their body. That didn't help me or my self-confidence, however, I tried to change as much as possible but it just didn't happen. I was so thin.

We hadn't made love for months, maybe just once, here and there, which was unusual but, to be honest, I was glad. I needed the rest, partly because I knew my body looked awful which made me step back a little. I didn't let Peter see me undressed because of how thin I was.

My hair was never the same either because quite a bit had fallen out over the months. I went to the hairdresser and had it restyled to suit what was left. That's probably the biggest thing that hurt me. I always had a really good head of hair and always looked after it. I remember Peter telling me on several occasions to stop wearing my hair up as he liked it down. But when I wore my hair up, it was beautiful and people always complimented my hair when I wore it up.

We talked about why he wanted a divorce and he told me that he had been depressed for some time. He thought the reason was because I resented him. I knew he had been feeling a little down and he said he had been talking to a counsellor about it. This was true because, at one time, she wanted to speak to me on my own. I wasn't too happy about it, but felt if I went to see her maybe she could touch on what was making Peter feel this way.

I remember I broke down in tears when we talked of the operation, which shocked me, but looking back I think maybe it was me who needed a counsellor. She told me that she couldn't discuss what she and Peter had talked about, but wanted to know my feelings so, for me, this was a waste of time. The funny thing was she too was Scottish.

However, Peter's meetings with her didn't last for long as he felt they were a waste of time. I think maybe he seen her around four times, but back then he told me he had been seeing her for months. I soon found out where he really was on his so-called meetings.

I suggested to him that maybe we should have a little time apart and he would have time to think if he really wanted a divorce, but he was adamant that he did and he didn't want time apart. He wanted me to leave as soon as possible.

I told him that, if that was what he really wanted, I would leave by the end of the following month. After that, those last weeks were pretty much a blur, I went to work as normal. I gave my notice which was a shock to Pam. She said to me, "Belinda, are you sure you want to hand in your notice, you can find somewhere to live and not move back to Scotland, you love it here."

I had no choice really. Yes, I could have stayed but without Peter how was I going to function? I know I had friends but I really didn't want to be a burden to anyone. I guess that's what comes with having an independent mind and being a little stubborn.

My other friends were surprised too, but they arranged a leaving night for me at one of the local pubs in Ponty, which was just up the street from where I worked.

13
Think Twice

I arranged to stay with Pam that night, because the village I lived in was miles away and there was no chance Peter would have come pick me up after a night out. In fact, I hadn't even told him I was going out. I decided that, if our marriage was over, I no longer needed to ask him for permission to do anything. I would just go ahead and do it.

I have to admit I was so looking forward to that night out and, boy, did I get drunk. It struck me that that's what I had been lacking; the company of people who wanted to dance and have fun, so fun I had.

Peter had told his parents that the marriage was over and, to be honest, I can't help thinking they were glad, more so his father. No matter how hard I tried, I could never seem to get inside that man's head. Don't get me wrong, he came to except all that had happened with his son and his marriage before me, but I could never seem to step into the footsteps of his ex-daughter-in-law.

Peter's father was a hard nut to crack, his mum, on the other hand, was a little on the softer side; although I wouldn't want to mess with her either. His sister and I got on really well, and I liked her a lot. We had many a laugh when I stayed at her house it was a shame that we didn't keep in touch after her brother and I ended our marriage. If I saw any of them in street, I would still say Hi even to Peter. I have forgiven him for everything but I will never forget, that's for sure. It's easy to forgive when a past grievance brings you to a place of complete happiness where you feel at peace, which is where I am now, but that is a whole new story!

It was the night of my leaving party and there were quite a few of my friends there, including some of the staff, and I couldn't have been happier or more excited, not because I was leaving, of course, but because I was able to spend time with friends and really let my hair down, or what was left of it! *'Smiling'*

I forgot what it was like to have quality time with friends. Back home in Scotland I was the devoted girl-friend and mother who stayed home and cleaned the house which, don't get me wrong, I loved. I was never one to go out partying and get drunk all the time.

I suppose there was an element of the child still in me; I didn't have what one would call an amazing child-hood, certainly not one to brag about that's for sure. I didn't know much other than school, cleaning and, even-tually, working to pay my parents what they needed for the burden of having me as a child. (Yep, you'll read all about that too, in my next book.)

I'm not sure if it was the fact that I was going out and had that feeling of excitement that made me go that extra mile when getting dressed, but I sure did look smart. I suppose, looking back, I hadn't been making much of an effort lately due to the illness and losing so much weight. I did always look my best when going to work though, that's one thing that didn't change but, at home, I didn't make such an effort.

I came out of the bath, wrapping the towels around, me as you do, one for my body and the other on my head. I looked in the mirror to apply my make-up and I let out this almighty scream. Pam ran to the bathroom door, "Belinda, you okay? Belinda… "

I opened the door and said to her, "I have just seen two grey hairs at the front of my hair."

"Oh my God," she said, "is that all?"

"What do you mean, is that all? Two is enough!"

She burst into a fit of laughter and said, "No, that's not what I meant, I thought by the sound of your scream something was seriously wrong."

"Yes, it is," I said, "I have two grey hairs." I still laugh to this day when I think of that night.

Before we went out to meet everyone we were chilling listening to music and having a few drinks to get us in the mood. We heard a knock at the door and when my friend opened it, I could hear her say, "Hello, Jai, what are you doing here?"

Jai, was one of the builders who did some jobs for us at my place of work. He and a couple of others called Ray and Patrick, who had become really good friends to both me and Pam. We had some laughs over the years and, I think, if it weren't for them, I would have gone insane while my marriage was on the rocks.

He asked Pam if he could have a chat with me. "Not at all," she said, "I will leave you both in the kitchen and close the door."

He then said to my friend, "Here take this CD, can you put it on and play this song, but turn it up." I wondered why would he want the music turned up. Pam took the CD and went into the other room. Jai, then picked me up, sat me on the work surface and kissed me. I remember feeling butterflies in my stomach but I'm not sure if that was excitement, mixed with the alcohol, or worry as to why he had just done that.

Next thing the song he had asked Pam to play came on, 'Think Twice' by Celine Dion. I started to say something but he stopped me and said, "Belinda, listen to the words until the end." We both listened and, although I was hearing some of the words, I was still trying to figure out what he was playing at. It wasn't until some months later after listening to that song over and over did I realise what he had been trying to tell me.

He had always had a thing for me and, as much as I liked him, he was married so it was a no go from the start. Which was a shame because, like any young girl, when someone handsome pays you a lot of attention, it is tempting to go for it. I will say, I have had many admirers and yes, I have kissed quite a few, including married men, but there was no chance of it developing into anything else. I suppose, like many people, when you are young you will kiss many a frog before you eventually end up with your prince.

The song finished and he took me in his arms. As he slowly brought me down from the counter, while kissing me, I could feel this rush of excitement and that kiss lasted a long time. I was feeling quite tipsy at this point so I was enjoying the moment.

Then he said to me, "I will see you at the pub in a bit and when you come home tonight play that song again before you go to sleep and listen to the words carefully." Then he left.

Pam came into the kitchen when she heard the door close and she was looking at me with this, 'Oh yes, and what was that all about kind of smile'. I didn't really know.

"Tell me all," she said. "I listened to the words of that song and, if my instincts are correct, then I think he was trying to tell you something."

"Oh yes, judging by the way he kissed me, I think so too."

"He kissed you? Tell me what did he say?"

"He told me to listen to the song again before I go to sleep tonight and listen carefully."

"Well, that confirms it," said my friend, "I told you months ago I thought he had a thing for you. Have you kissed him before?"

"Yes, well, I didn't... he kissed me about four weeks ago when I was in the warehouse. I was putting the last delivery of documents in alphabetical order and one fell on my foot, it was extremely heavy and I let out a yelp. He came over and asked if I was all right. I said that I would be fine. Then went to pick up the file at the same time as me and he looked me square in the face and kissed me."

"You didn't tell me about that."

"I know, I couldn't because it was wrong and I didn't want you to tease me about it."

14
Marriage of Convenience

Jai, and I had been attracted to one another for quite some time. He had been doing jobs at the factory with the other men, on and off for a couple of years. We always got on well and had many a laugh, just messing around really, but that soon turned physical; you know the odd brush past me, but meaning to bump against me, things like that.

It had probably been going on for a while but I just didn't see what was happening, I'm a little slow that way I have to say. Later on, though, I did come to realise that he was purposely brushing against me or standing too close. I tried to ignore it but, at the same time, I also got a bit of a kick out of it. I think it was because I was getting the attention that I should have had from Peter.

After Jai, and I had that kiss in the warehouse, I did have him on my mind from time to time but I soon came down to earth when I thought of my husband, at the end of the day it was him that I loved and I would not stray.

I suppose having a kiss with another man *is* straying in a sense but I didn't think it was back then because I never slept with anyone else. I have, however, had many a kiss and was not short of admirers. I could have had my choice of many men who had a thing for me but I didn't take them up.

Knowing what I know now I guess, in a sense, that I am like my father; my biological father. This is another thing you will read about, and what a shocker that was, not to mention other revelations in the last four years that have basically torn me in half. That will be in my next book.

Meanwhile, back to that night; the pub was buzzing and the music in full flow. What an amazing atmosphere, you could hardly move as my friend and I made our way through the hordes of people to find the rest of the group.

There they were all sat by the table, some standing and some still to arrive, by this time I was half cut and feeling on a high. I could see Jai, as soon as I got to the table and my stomach was doing summersaults. *Oh my, I know that feeling* I thought to myself. *I need to keep my wits about me.*

We drank we danced and as the night went on I got more and more drunk. Not something had I planned to do, but I remember thinking how much courage I had when I had a drink and it made me feel good. I was always a quiet girl with not a lot of confidence so when I had a drink I made the most of it, and I've always known exactly what I'm doing when I've had one too many.

Jai, and I danced for a bit and then he asked me to go outside so he could talk to me, so off we went. He took me in his arms and said to me, "Belinda, please don't leave." I said that I had no choice as I had nowhere to go and he said he would find me a place so that I could stay in Wales.

Before I could say anything he pulled me closer and started kissing me, by this time I was pretty much well gone and enjoyed every minute, not giving his wife a second thought, well, most people wouldn't when they are, basically, pissed.

He said that he had had feelings for me for some time, but before I could say a word the door of the pub opened and he stepped back. It was Ray, he walked over to us and Jai, went back in the pub.

Ray told me that he had a friend who had a string of flats and he could set one up for me if I wanted to stay. "I really appreciate the thought, Ray, but I can't have you going out of your way like that and, besides, these places cost a small fortune and I don't make that kind of money at the factory."

That was true, back then it wasn't even minimum wage. I was only paid £75 a week and a flat would have easily set me back about £250 a month. I wouldn't have been able to eat.

"Well, none of us want you to leave, so please think about it and let me know. I can manage to help pay some of your rent until you find another job."

I wasn't surprised that Ray had offered me this opportunity as he had his own business and he too, had a thing for me. He sat with me one lunchtime and asked me if I was happy as he could see I was going through a difficult time in my marriage. I was truthful with him and told him that I was having problems but I didn't go into detail. I've always tried to be as private as possible except when I had no choice.

He said to me that day, "Belinda, I've been in a love-less marriage for many years and, although my wife and I share the business, I would be willing to give it up to be with you." Never in my life have I been so dumbfounded as I was right then.

He was an older man, probably old enough to be my dad, and it's not like I ever looked on him that way. He was being absolutely serious and I couldn't even speak for a moment. When I did, I said to him, "Ray you are a really lovely man I am extremely grateful to have you as a friend and flattered that you want to be with me but I can't look at you that way you'll always be just a friend."

I felt a little sorry saying it that way but I had to be truthful I couldn't give him any reason to think otherwise but after all that, we are still good friends to this day. Believe me, there are not many friends who have stuck by me after being knocked back, but those who have mean the world to me and me to them.

So, I said I would think about it but it was doubtful I would stay. By this time Leanne was on my mind. I may have been drunk and enjoying myself and the kisses from Jai but before I knew it reality hit me.

This is my last night with everyone I know, I thought, *I'm going back to Scotland, I won't be able to pick up where I left off but I will be with my daughter so I'm going to make sure I enjoy the rest of this night to the fullest.*

We went back into the pub the drinking and dancing continued. I was very drunk, but not so drunk as not to know what I was doing, thank goodness, and what an amazing night it was, full of singing, dancing, laughter and lots of tears.

The night had come to an end, some wanted to go back to one of the girl's homes and continue to party but I knew by now that I had enough and wanted to sleep, as I've always done when I've had way too much alcohol.

I went up to Pam's daughter's room where I was staying. Her daughter was staying at another friend's house that night because she was young and we would be late back. It never entered my head to listen to Jai's song; I was so tired.

I woke with Pam asking me if I wanted breakfast before or after my shower, I said after. I so enjoyed that shower but what a hangover I had, I hadn't had that much to drink since I worked at The Silver Fox.

In fact, from the time I broke up with Michael until a couple of months before me and Peter got together, I was quite dependent on drink. It seemed my only escape from my past and the only thing that would get me through those terrible months.

I was in the room with towels wrapped around me, putting my clothes on the bed to get ready when there was a knock at the door. "Is breakfast ready? I will be down in a couple of minutes," I called out.

The door slowly opened and I got the shock of my life when I turned around to see Jai, standing there. "Sorry, Belinda, Pam told me just to come up. I stood there in shock thinking, *I've just got out of the shower and I have no make-up on and he is stood right here.*

Without another word he came over to me, took me in his arms and kissed me again, only this time there was so much passion that went into it I thought I was actually in heaven. I could not contain myself and kissed him passionately too.

I really did feel the earth move, in fact the last time it had been like that was with my husband. My husband what on earth was I doing? I was married but that didn't seem to stop me. It was as if I wanted to stop, but couldn't, and I often wonder if I allowed this to happen because I needed the affection or because I was falling for him?

Before I knew it, he was slowly caressing me and it felt good, and I had this rush of, what I can only describe as, pins and needles from my stomach to my heart.

The next thing we were in bed and making love. We lay there for a long time after and for the first five minutes or so we didn't speak, then he said to me, "Belinda, please don't go. I have fallen in love with you."

"Jai, you are married," I said, "and so am I come to that."

"But your marriage is over," he said, "and as for me, I will leave her. My marriage is just a convenience anyway and has been for a long time." This I knew to be true because Patrick was Jai's brother-in-law and he had told me that his sister and Jai's marriage was a sham.

"I can't, Jai. I really do like you a lot and I know that my marriage is over. If you were single then things might be different, but you're not, and I can't do it."

"I will leave her first, then. You stay in Wales, I will leave my wife and eventually we can be together."

It all sounded good but in the real world I knew it wouldn't be that simple. I had my daughter to think about now and I wasn't about to stay in Wales knowing that there was a good future ahead of me with her if I went back (or so I thought).

He said, "If you really feel you need to go back to Scotland then so be it, but I am leaving my wife anyway and we can keep in touch. Who knows what the future may hold? You may change your mind."

"Okay, I said I will keep that thought," I said, knowing deep down it wasn't going to happen.

We went downstairs and he stayed long enough for a cup of tea then left. Pam asked me what had happened. I told her and she asked me what I was going to do.

"I can't do it, Pam, you know the score. I have too much going on in my life right now to be starting over already and, besides, how do I know that he is telling me the truth about him and his wife."

Later that day I made my way back home to the village. I had the CD that Jai, gave me at least I could listen to that song and remember him with fondness.

15
Hate in his Eyes

When I walked in the door, Peter stood there and looked at me with hate in his eyes.

"Where have you been?"

"Its none of your bloody business where I've been remember, I don't owe you any explanations anymore. You made yourself clear when you told me to leave."

He was raging by this point, "You still live in this house and, until you leave, I have a right to know where you have been."

"REALLY," I said, "somehow I don't think so. If it means that much to you, I was out with people who care about me who don't want me to go back to Scotland. My friends!"

I thought to myself, *keep calm Belinda don't start shouting and making things worse.* It didn't work by this time; I was the one in control and I told him everything… well, everything except what happened with Jai. If I had told him about Jai, he would most definitely have pulled the trigger on that gun of his this time.

The rest of the day went by without any blips other than Peter giving me the odd look of disgust that I had been out all night. What made me laugh was the fact that he was a man who thought he could have it all. He wanted a divorce yet the thought of me being with another man made him furious.

I carried on packing more of my stuff and bagging the things that had to go in the bin. Before I knew it, it was nine thirty in the evening. I went downstairs to the living room to burn some items in the coal fire, that way I was sure they were destroyed and nobody could get hold of them.

Peter was sitting there and asked what I was burning. I told him it was our wedding video and some of the outfits that we had bought, outfits that some woman wear when we have those periods of 'let's dress up and get excited'. You know the type I mean.

He was really angry and tried to stop me. "Why would you want to burn them?" he said.

I looked at him, before saying in a horrible tone, "Do you think I'm going to leave these here for your next woman to use? Get a grip."

I honestly will never understand Peter at all; he thought it was okay to end our marriage, yet leave behind the naughty stuff, so he can what? Reminisce… Hell no!

I had one week left at work and only a couple of days after that before I left for Scotland. I called Leanne and told her that I was coming back for good. I also spoke to Michael and put him in the picture. I was actually amazed at the fact he spoke to me with an element of kindness for a change, a little like how it used to be. My daughter was extremely excited too and that made it all the more pleasant for me.

The weekend seemed to drag on, unfortunately, because my husband didn't go out much.

Maybe he thought I might take something of his. Fat chance! I wanted nothing but my personal belongings and the rest he could shove where the sun didn't shine.

It was Sunday and there was no dinner for me to cook. I wasn't about to cook a Sunday roast as if nothing was wrong. There was a knock at the door, it was Robert; his father owned a local repair shop and both Peter and I had become good friends with him.

I opened the door, "Hi, Balou," he said, that was his nickname for me.

"Hi, how's things?" I responded. "Come in. I can't stop, I'm upstairs packing. Peter is through there."

"What are you packing for, are you off on holiday?"

"You could call it that. Peter will tell you all about it, I'm sure. He is in the kitchen." I could just about hear their conversation from the room upstairs but had to listen really carefully to actually hear what Peter was saying. I was inquisitive to know how he would explain to Robert that it was over between us, as we hadn't seen him in a few months.

I heard Robert say, "No way."

Peter said, "Yes, I just can't do it."

"Come on, you know you don't really want this, you love her. When is she going?" asked Robert?

'Two weeks'

"Right, Peter, you have two weeks. You need to think long and hard, I don't think you want to do this."

"I have no choice," Peter replied. "I don't want to as I really do love her but there's no other way." I couldn't hear much after that but I did think, *why the hell is Peter saying that he really loves me and doesn't want to do it, yet he has no choice?*

I came in from work the next day and asked him, "Are you having an affair?"

Peter said, "No!"

So, you love me, yet you're letting me go, I think that there is more to this than you are admitting." I asked his friends over the next few days and even spoke to his sister and they were adamant that he wasn't having an affair. I just couldn't get my head round it.

The next few days in work was as pleasant as could be. Jai, and Ray both came in those last few days and asked me if I had changed my mind about leaving I told them that I hadn't. So. on the Friday, they came to the factory as Pam had arranged for everyone to give me a gift and card to remember them by and we all had lunch. It was a special kind of day but also very emotional for me. I tried so hard not to cry again.

I told Pam I would be back on and off to visit as I felt Wales was my home and I couldn't just walk away forever. The weekend dragged so much I wanted it to hurry and be Monday, I had butterflies in my stomach but not the nice kind. It was the fear setting in that now the time had come and there was no going back.

Peter's dad had paid for a van for me and my stuff to be transported back to Scotland; I don't think he could wait to see the back of me. God only knows what my husband had told him as to why it had all ended.

16
The Journey Back to Scotland

Peter's friend, Steve, drove the van and when he came to pick me up I crumbled. I watched as Peter stood at the door, I was looking for a hint that he may change his mind but he didn't.

Even when we left the village, I thought he might come after me, I kept watching the mirror for the car, but nothing. The weird thing is on that drive back to Scotland a song came on the radio, Tom Jones 'The Green, Green Grass'. Yep, I broke down and cried my eyes out. It was the very same song from the day I first arrived in Wales. Poor Steve just didn't know what to say.

That journey back to Scotland took a long, long time, which wasn't such a good thing because I had too much time to think. Everything I had gone through; with Michael, then moving to Wales, now back to my parents' home where I had grown up. I had left in the first place because I was no longer prepared to say, 'how high?' every time others said, 'Jump!'

By that I mean being the black sheep of the family. As I was the oldest, sadly, it was me who got all the hidings for the stupidest things, it was me who had to stay indoors while my brother and sisters got to be out with their friends, while I was washing the windows or helping to clean the house.

I took many a hiding for being as little as five minutes late home and I was always shouted at by my parents.

I was so envious of all my friends as they got to stay out past 7:00 p.m. of an evening while I had to be home and in bed by 8 o'clock. Looking back what a life I had.

I had wanted to leave home to be me, I didn't want to continue to live a life where I felt unloved or where I would get the odd smack for saying or doing something normal. We arrived at the house and unloaded the van, which didn't take too long.

If I remember correctly Steve didn't even stay for a cup of tea, he wanted to drive straight back home. He must have felt shattered by the time he got back to Wales because we left around 7:00 p.m. and it's a four and a half hour drive without a stop, so to drive straight back must have been very tiring. I wouldn't have done it, that's for sure.

All my stuff was put in the room upstairs and I got changed and went to sleep on the sofa in the living room. I was very tired but, at the same time, I didn't want questions fired at me about how this had all come about. I was afraid I would cry and that is one thing I would never let my family see ever again.

I suppose I had hardened myself as when I was younger and lived with them they were so tough on me, I was the only one out of the five of us who was hit on a regular basis. I suppose nowadays it would be called child abuse.

I always felt different and years later I found out why.

I tried to talk to my mum the next day about what had happened between me and Peter but, as usual, she didn't show any interest, nor was she even listening to what I was saying so I dropped it. Instead I went for a walk and cried until there were no more tears left.

I was determined I wouldn't go back on the drink, which is something I did after Michael and I split up. I drank all the time, trying to block out what had happened and the fact that he and his mother took my daughter and wouldn't let me see or speak to her again.

I had a lawyer to take care of everything which proved to be a total waste of time and money. I had to pay him just under £300 to send three letters to my ex, which was a struggle because I worked and couldn't get legal aid. Someone advised me to give up my job so that I could get legal aid. So I did, only to find out that I wasn't eligible for benefits because I was the one who ended my job.

So, no job, no benefits, therefore no legal aid! I didn't have a leg to stand on.

I found another job soon after, and I worked my socks off, back shift and night shift but I was young and I could stand the pace. I've always been a grafter but I was still drinking and I would go out with friends and return home to my parents drunk. One day, my dad said to me, "The best thing you can do, is go away live somewhere else and start again. Leanne is in school now and you don't want to mess her head up by fighting for her." I thought, *yes, I will move away and soon after get custody of her,* how wrong I was.

That was the one and only time I listened to my dad and I regretted it years later. My dad and I never did see eye to eye and I think it was his way of saying, "You're in our way, so go." It all fell into place years later and now I knew for sure that they resented me although I don't think my mother actually realised it. Maybe I was a constant reminder of my biological father? I don't think I will ever know.

I wasn't back in Scotland very long before I went back down to Wales for a couple of days and going back made me realise just how much I missed living there. I popped to the factory to see Pam and the girls, and as I walked through the door I felt like I hadn't been away and I was turning up for work.

A little later I was chatting to one of the girls when she said to me, "I'm really sorry about what happened between you and Peter. I kind of wish I hadn't known what was going on because it was hard to keep it from you." By this point she obviously thought I knew.

At that moment I knew there was something I hadn't been told before, I decided to let her think I already knew and said to her, "Don't worry, I understand, although I just wish he had of come clean at the time." Deep down I kind of had a feeling he had been seeing someone but didn't let on to her so that she would tell me what she knew.

I said that I would just like to know where he found the time because he was always with me except when working. She told me that he would go and see her before he went to work in the morning. Right then my stomach felt like it fallen out and hit the floor, looking back that explained why he left for work an hour earlier every morning for several weeks. He told me that they had a contract that required them to work earlier and be home a little later.

How foolish was I? Never once did I think he was, or had been, cheating on me because he was so possessive in our marriage.

At that point all I wanted to do was curl up and die, to think that Peter had been sleeping with someone else, then coming into bed with me made me feel sick. I said that I wanted to know who she was but he wouldn't tell me.

"Belinda," said my colleague, "it was Lindsay," as if I knew her.

"Lindsay who?"

"You remember, she worked here a long time ago." I racked my brain but still couldn't remember her. She told me that Lindsay lived in Bryn Deri but I still didn't know who she was.

Anyhow, right then I didn't care but the fact that the truth had finally come out had me in a foul mood and all I wanted to do was confront him. What made it worse was the fact that I had asked his friends and family at the time they all said he wasn't having an affair.

I left the factory soon after and got the bus to my old home. Peter wasn't back from work as the car wasn't in the drive, so I waited at his uncle's house. His uncle could tell that I knew, as it was written all over his face. Eventually, I saw the car come into the street from the window, but as I got up to go and confront him, his uncle said, "I will go and let Peter know you are here." I wasn't giving him that chance and refused.

He was locking up the car as I approached the drive, he looked round saw me and his face was as white as a sheet. I knew right then he was worried and so he should have been. I didn't wait to be invited in; I told him that as far as I was concerned the house was still mine until we divorced, what a cheek, but I didn't care at this point.

I went straight to the kitchen, switched the kettle on and said to him, "You don't mind if I make a sandwich? I'm rather hungry."

"Why are you here?" he said.

"WHY? I will tell you why, tell me about Lindsay…" You could have heard a pin drop to the floor after that and for a few minutes there was silence. Eventually he asked how I knew? I told him not to worry about that and to tell me his side of the story.

I asked him how he met her and what the attraction had been. He said she worked as a cook at our local pub. Again I asked, Why? What has she got that I didn't?

"Big breasts," he replied. (I too, had big breasts before I got ill and lost a ton of weight.)

To that I said, "You can't be serious, you ended our marriage for bigger breasts," and I laughed out loud but inside I was heartbroken.

He said, "You need to go as Lindsay will be on her way here now."

"Really," I replied, "then I'm not going anywhere. I want to see this wench with the big breasts." I was fuming.

Then the panic set in, he was all over the place, "No, Belinda, please don't cause any trouble."

"TROUBLE! You don't know the meaning of the word but you're sure about to find out," I said. He was in a terrible state and called his friend to ask him to come round to the house right now. There was a knock on the door and his friend was there. Peter spoke to him and invited him in. The next thing he said was, "I need to go and collect the kids from my dad's, I will be back in a second," (his father lived just around the corner) and he left his friend with me.

Around ten minutes later he returned but with no kids in tow. I asked where they were and said that I would like to see them. He told me that he had lied and he only said that so that he could tell Lindsay not to come to the house.

"Her moment will come," I said, getting up. I think he was panicking that I would hang around the village because he offered me a lift back to Pam's, which, of course, I accepted but only to save paying a huge taxi fare.

17
She's Pregnant

We didn't speak much on the journey and, during the little that was said, I asked him what was so bad about our marriage that he felt the need to stray. In the end I cried which did make him feel bad; I could see it in his eyes.

We got to Pam's which was at the top of the hill near the Panorama and he stopped the car just around the corner. He said he was so sorry for what he done and that didn't mean to hurt me.

I asked, "Why then? If you didn't want to hurt me why didn't you end the marriage before taking up with her?"

He said that it had just happened and that he had been feeling low for a long time after my operation. I wasn't prepared for his next move, he said to me, "Do you want to drive further up for old time's sake?"

"How dare you," I raged at him. "You sleep with another woman, end our marriage and now you want to have your way with me 'for old time's sake'? Not likely, you can fuck off." At that point I got out of the car and slammed the door closed. That was the last I heard from him until a few months later.

I wasn't long out of bed after my night shift when the phone rang, I asked my brother to answer it as I was in the middle of making a cup of tea. A second later, he said, "Belinda, it's for you."

I asked who it was and he covered the phone and said, "I think its Peter." I wondered why he would be calling me after our last meeting a couple of months earlier; my heart was beating fast I wasn't sure if maybe, he was calling to ask me to come back. I was still brokenhearted that we were no longer together and I did miss him, even though he done the unthinkable.

"Hello," I said, pretending not to know who it was.

"Belinda…" then there was a pause for a long time. "There is something I think you need to know." Right then I knew what was coming next. I could tell by the tone of his voice that it was something that would upset me. "It's Lindsay, she's pregnant."

I felt my knees go weak, my legs shook and I felt sick. I hung up the phone and I broke my heart like never before. My brother knew that whatever Peter had said must have been bad because he had never seen me so upset. He didn't speak to me, instead he gave me the space I needed. I ran upstairs and cried my eyes out.

Around fifteen minutes later the phone rang again, this time my brother let me answer it as he must have sensed it would be Peter again.

"Belinda, are you okay?" Peter asked.

I couldn't speak for a second, then I said to him in a calm voice, through my tears. "What do you think?"

"I'm so sorry," he said, "I didn't want this to happen."

All I could say was, "You made me get sterilised and now you have got another woman pregnant?"

"Belinda, I really didn't want this. I was shocked when she told me; it was an accident."

Then I got angry and said, "Didn't you think to put something on the end of it?"

"There's nothing more I can say, Belinda, I'm sorry."

At that point I told him that I was filing for a divorce on the grounds of adultery. He started to panic, saying, "No, Belinda, please you can't do that."

"Just watch me," I said, then hung up the phone.

Before we separated we both went to see a lawyer who advised us to wait two years before applying for our divorce as sometimes people change their minds. He said that he didn't get the feeling that we both wanted to divorce at that stage and yes, he was right, I didn't, and although, at the beginning, Peter did, he never said he wanted it to happen right away. We took his advice.

Now, though, it was different; I wanted that divorce from him because, as far as I was concerned, he was a lying, cheating, irresponsible swine and It was payback time. Now, I badly wanted to hurt him. When Peter told me that Lindsay was expecting his child it was like the knife he stuck in me was being twisted right in my heart. He had already hurt me but this was like pushing the knife further in.

I saw the lawyer not long after and got the ball rolling, I didn't want to waste any more time on him or his bit on the side. The quicker I got him out of my life the better.

The one thing I regret the most was feeling sorry for Lindsay, when I said I was divorcing him on the grounds of adultery he begged me not to mention her name. He said it would be in the papers and she wouldn't be able to handle it.

I saw my lawyer and he advised me to have a private investigator go to his house and ask for me. The lawyer said they would have a photo of me so that when she came to the door they could then say, this is not her. Then they wouldn't be able to deny the adultery.

Peter begged me not to do it and, feeling sorry for a pregnant woman, I decided not to go ahead. I explained why to my lawyer. He also told me I was entitled to half

Peter's pension and, with Welsh law, even though I was in Scotland and we had no children together, Peter would have to keep me until I married again. I simply told him, no way. I want nothing from him.

A couple of months later, I was back in Wales for a few days. I stayed at Pam's and Peter came to see me. He said that Lindsay had moved in with him and with her being pregnant he couldn't afford the court costs but needed the divorce.

He asked me to let him divorce me on the grounds of adultery. You can imagine how angry I was and said no as I had done nothing wrong. He almost broke his heart and, yet again, I felt sorry for him. After chatting for a few hours, I gave in. I said, "Okay, do what you have to do but I will never forgive you for this." That was most definitely the biggest mistake I ever made.

18
An Abusive Relationship

I carried on working and, by this time, I was back in touch with Michael. We were on talking terms and he had left his girlfriend around the time of my going back to Scotland. The funny thing is, we started to see each other on a regular basis, and eventually decided to give things another go.

I had always loved my daughter's father, although I wasn't in love with him. I think, looking back, subconsciously I thought, because I still loved him, it might work out and we could be a family again. I would also have Leanne back in my life full time.

That though, was just a flash in the pan and it didn't last long. It was the guilt; his ex-girlfriend, who had a son by him, was expecting and later gave birth to a daughter. I didn't feel good, I thought, *I have just had this done to me and I cannot do this to her.* I had to back off and, not wanting to hurt him, I made the excuse that I was missing Wales and wanted to go back. He said he would move there with me, so in the end I had to come clean.

I told him that I couldn't do to his ex what I had just had done to me and I wanted him to sort things out with her. I knew it meant losing my daughter all over again but I had no choice because her grandmother told me that Leanne said she would run away if her father and I stayed together.

Later, I came to realise that she was being brain-washed and Leanne hadn't thought that way, never mind said it. I was so young, stupid and naive back then, if only I knew then what I know now!

I found myself a job and a house in Wales and moved back there soon after. I felt good about myself and that I was back in control of my life. Eventually, I started dating someone who was a close friend of mine, Andrew, but that was a weird relationship. I was definitely on the rebound when I started dating him. Andrew was around four years younger than me and I think what attracted me to him was that glint in his eye. It was a relationship destined to fail.

Andrew beat me on several occasions for which I had him arrested by the police but, each time, I dropped the charges and took him back. Again, he would beat me and it wasn't just physical abuse, it was mental too. One night after an argument and him taking a knife to me, he later said sorry and tried to sweet talk me, but I wasn't interested in his apologies anymore; they meant nothing.

Later that same night, in bed, Andrew wanted to make love. I said that I didn't want to, but he wouldn't take no for an answer. I just lay there crying but he carried on. The next day there was another big argument and he threw me out of my house barefoot. I ran to a friend's house and called the police and, while waiting for them, I hid in the bushes in case he came looking for me. I really didn't want my friends to be dragged into our fight.

I told the police I was in the bushes and they told me to stay there until they arrived which I did. They drove to my house but parked at the corner and stayed with me while another car arrived and the police went into the house and arrested him.

I couldn't sleep that night until the police told me Andrew would be locked up all weekend and appear in court on the Monday morning. I was so relieved he was away from me; this time I was going ahead with the charges.

The next day a police officer and a doctor came to the house. I was in a terrible state and so ill with worry, I didn't know what to do. The officer said that I should go into sheltered housing so that he wouldn't know where I was, but I refused. Why should I leave my home? He should go back to where he came from (Andrew wasn't from Wales).

The officer left and the doctor waited to talk to me on my own. I broke down in tears and told him everything that had happened over the months since my meeting him. I told him that he made love to me when I didn't want to. The doctor asked if I had told him that I didn't want to?

I said, "Yes! I was crying but he just carried on."

The doctor then said to me, "He didn't make love to you, Belinda, he raped you."

"NO! He didn't," I said, "I know him, he didn't pull me by the hair and rip my clothes off." "The doctor replied, Belinda, the majority of victims who are raped know the person who has done it. He doesn't have to drag you kicking and screaming by the hair to rape you. The fact is that you were crying and said no and he carried on regardless. He raped you.

By this time I was in pieces and was advised that, if I didn't go into a shelter, my life could be at risk. I still said no, because I was charging him this time. I told the doctor that I needed something to calm my nerves, but he refused and said that in a case like this, he could not give me anything.

"I think you are suffering from depression," he continued, "but you need to talk to someone before I can prescribe you pills."

Maybe he thought that I might decide to end my life (I have to admit, it did cross my mind on occasion when Andrew had beaten me); I thought there was no other way out at the time. On the Sunday, I had a phone call from a friend of Andrew's, who said he had to pass a message; if you charge him he will have someone come and sort you out once and for all. That was it; I had to drop the charges again, for fear of my life. I was stuck; what else could I do?

On the Monday, I stayed home. I was afraid to go to work because, on one occasion when Andrew and I argued, he went back to his hometown only to travel back to Wales the next day when I was at work and broke into my house. I stayed at home this time, just in case.

The phone rang that afternoon and it was him. He said that he had been told to go back to his hometown and not to come anywhere near me but that he wanted me to meet him at the train station just to talk. This time I said no! He asked me again, said that he was sorry and again I said no. After which, he then said, "Okay, bitch, you're going to get what's coming to you, I'm coming for you now." (The reason I wouldn't go to the train station was because I actually had a vision of him throwing me in front of a train.)

I dropped the phone, called the police and told them what Andrew had said and that he was on his way to get me. Within minutes, four officers arrived; two stayed with me in the house and there was one at the front and one at the back door. Another two officers drove towards Llanharen where they found Andrew on his way to mine. Again he was arrested.

I called one of my friends, back in Scotland, who hired a van and came up the next day with my dad to take me home. That was the quickest I have ever packed a house full of my belongings to move away.

Andrew called me some months later and I told him in no uncertain terms that I couldn't be sure he would get out of Scotland without a mark. There were friends of mine who would have had pleasure in giving him a taste of what he gave me.

19
Back to Wales

Something else really upset me, I was in a shop in town and who did I bump into? Peter and his pregnant girl-friend. Lindsay was around eight months gone so you can imagine the horror I felt. To make it worse, I had a black eye from one of the beatings Andrew had given me. I hated that my ex-husband had seen it.

That day in the shop when I saw Lindsay and how far gone she was, I was in bits. I can't begin to describe how terrible that made me feel. She was carrying the baby I should have had.

On the one hand, I felt like I was going to be physically sick, on the other, I wanted to walk over to Peter and punch him, and give her a slap for good measure. If she hadn't been pregnant, I would have done for sure. That was the last time I saw Peter, although he called me when I was back in Scotland to ask if we could try again.

What a bloody cheek, I thought, after he sleeps with another woman, or should I say, young girl, as she is around eight, maybe ten, years younger than him and gets her pregnant.

Mind, that wasn't the only time Peter had been unfaithful; a couple of years after we were married he told me that once, when he worked away from home, he had had an affair with a woman while he was married to his ex-wife.

It's quite sad really, as for years after we split I made excuses, saying it was down to me being ill and losing weight. Slowly, though, I began to realise that he just couldn't keep it in his trousers. I do still think I'm a little to blame; after all, he liked a curvy woman there I was just under seven stone!

I've been told over the years that Peter has had a number of other affairs. Needless to say, he did the same thing to Lindsay and they ended up getting divorced. I do feel sorry for her because he left her with two children.

What a sad life! Don't get me wrong, when we were together for the first couple of years, it was amazing and we loved each other so much. Peter was a proper family man and looked after me well. Maybe too well, That's another reason why I found it hard on discovering that he had had an affair while we were married.

I always said, when I was younger, that I would love to live in the country in a nice little cottage. When Peter and I were married, we lived right next to a farm. That was my life complete; I had everything that I had dreamed of, and more, before it all came crashing down. The house actually belonged to my ex-father-in-law, who bought it after his mother passed away, so Peter and I rented it from him. Peter decided to buy it from his father after we split up; he had no choice really, as he got his mistress pregnant so he had to do the right thing by her.

I can't help but smile when I tell this part of the story because, I can just picture his father's face when his son and Lindsay split up and Peter had to sell the house and give her, her share.

His father would have been livid, no longer having his mother's home in the family. What is it they say, *'what goes around comes around'* Yep! Karma is a bitch.

I still would like to know what Peter told his parents about why we were getting a divorce, because that last few weeks his mother tried hard to avoid me. She must have thought I wasn't aware of it but it was clear as day. I didn't see much of his father that last few weeks either, he was, without a doubt, avoiding me too. I didn't really get the chance to say goodbye to our friends; I think they all felt they just didn't know what to say. I did, however, try to arrange to see my stepdaughters. I missed them.

I still go to Wales, but not as often as I would like to. One of my dearest friends passed away in 2006 and it hit me hard. It's just not the same when I go down there, knowing he is no longer around.

I'm still in touch with Pam and I go to visit her when I'm down and we talk on the phone from time to time. I'm also still close to what I call my 'other family', and I stay over with the daughter of my friend who passed away. I met them before he died; a lovely family and they have been kind enough to have me at their home when I go to Wales.

As for Jeff; that poor boy did indeed leave the village and went back home to London. I did get the chance to speak to him before he left, and he said that he didn't blame me for my boyfriend's failings. I often wonder if Peter ever said anything to Barry, because he knew we had a brief encounter. I never gave it a thought to ask Barry mind, I'm not sure he would have told me even if I had. As for Barry, he was by now married and had his own life and we only ever saw him here and there after that.

My life back home in Scotland is good. I'm getting on with things and I'v put the past behind me, or that part anyway. Almost three years after returning home to Scotland I was told the most disturbing news ever by my uncle, just when I thought there could be no more deceit…

Acknowledgments

My first thanks you goes to my oldest daughter's father, who respected me enough to wait, and for giving me the most precious gift of our relationship (our daughter). She has given me a handsome grandson and two beautiful granddaughters.

Yes, I'm going to thank my ex-husband, Peter; if it weren't for his cheating I wouldn't be where I am now. His loss – My gain!

I would like to thank Kim Kimber (www.kimkimber.co.uk), for copy editing my book and keeping me on track.

I would also like to thank photographer, Martin Sweeny, (www.knightshadesphotography.co.uk) for the cover photo of my book.

I have other people to thank or, perhaps not, as they are better suited to my second book *Secrets and Lies*. You will understand why after you have read it. I can promise you this next book is quite explosive.

Secrets and Lies

Well, back to Scotland I went, but it didn't end there. Now, I had a choice to make with two jobs on offer, in two different countries. Or should I stay in Scotland?

What happened next, was the biggest bombshell of all!

If you enjoyed this book then you are certain to enjoy the second one, *Secrets and Lies*. Read what happened next and how it affected me and those in my life.

Secrets and Lies will be on sale very soon.

Extracts of my next book *Secrets and Lies,* the sequel to *Sad, Lonely and a Long Way From Home* will be published on my website: insideoutlastyle.com

22987792R00091

Printed in Great Britain
by Amazon